What a feast of wonderful stories: the range he covers is quite amazing, from Hutton to Khashoggi, from Nixon to Tiny Rowland, from Bertrand Russell to Mohammed Ali; there's something to entertain everyone. Donald Trelford may well have edited the *Observer* in its glory days, but he is in truth an out of work sports editor, whose knowledge of almost every sport where a ball is involved is second to none. I delight in these pieces and know that anyone who picks up this book is in for a lot of fun.

Jeffrey Archer   January 2020

HEROES & VILLAINS

HEROES & VILLAINS

Donald Trelford

GALILEO PUBLISHERS

Published by Galileo Publishers
16 Woodlands Road, Great Shelford, Cambridge, UK, CB22 5LW
www.galileopublishing.co.uk
Galileo Publishers is an imprint of Galileo Multimedia Ltd.

USA: SCB Distributors
15608 S. New Century Drive Gardena, CA 90248-2129 | USA

Australia: Peribo Pty Ltd
58 Beaumont Rd, Mount Kuring-Gai, 2080 NSW, Australia

ISBN: 9781912916-27-6

Text design by RNH Associates

Cover Photo © Claire Trelford
Cover: NamdesignUK

Printed in the EU

In Memory of Tim Trelford (1966–2018)

CONTENTS:

7. COMRADES

8. FALLEN HEROES

INTRODUCTION

My first newspaper article was published in the *Observer* on 20 September,1959. It was a report of a rugby match between Coventry and Cardiff; in those days, before national leagues were formed, English and Welsh clubs routinely played each other. It was followed by several more match reports in that season, and the next, even though I was still an undergraduate at Cambridge. One of those reports opened with a quotation from *The Great Gatsby* by Scott Fitzgerald — "Reserving judgements is a matter of infinite hope" — an affectation that still makes me cringe after 60 years.

I was able to give up my Saturdays to report rugby matches because a broken arm and damaged ankle, sustained when I crashed a motorbike, had shattered what little chance I ever had of playing scrum-half for the university, or for anybody else for that matter.

So, I have written articles for the *Observer* in each of the seven decades from the 1950s to the 2010s — and that will become eight decades if the paper asks me to write one in the 2020s, which would surely create some kind of a record.

The idea of putting together a collection of articles from those 60 years in journalism began with a book I wrote in 2017 about my life in newspapers (*Shouting in the Street*, published by Biteback). The idea came from Brian MacArthur, an old friend and a highly respected journalist, who sadly died last year. He sent me an apologetic email to say that he had reviewed my book, describing it as "the most entertaining newspaper memoir since Harold Evans" — but, unfortunately, the *Daily Mail* had been unable to find space for his review.

He had picked up on some comments in the book by Gavin Young, the former *Observer* foreign correspondent, travel writer (and sometime agent of MI6), who had written a flattering article to mark my departure from the *Observer*. MacArthur suggested: "Why don't you republish some of your articles if they are as good as Gavin Young says they are? You are better known as an editor than a writer, but perhaps you might surprise us — or even surprise yourself!"

My immediate response was that I hadn't written anything like enough articles to justify a collection; I had always wished that I had written more for the *Observer*. Then, as it happens, at my wife's urging,

I started on the massive task of sorting the hundreds of papers, office memos, speeches (in 19 countries) and newspaper cuttings that I had kept in dozens of files, scrapbooks and boxes since I left the *Observer* in 1993 and had carried with me when we moved to Majorca ten years later. Her hope, a reasonable one, was that after completing my book I wouldn't need them anymore.

The volume of by-lined articles among this bulk amazed me, not just from the *Observer,* but from other newspapers and magazines; I couldn't even remember writing some of them. I was surprised to discover that I have written for every British newspaper, daily or Sunday (including the now defunct *News of the World*), except the *Sun*, the *Mirror* papers and the *Daily Star.* There were so very many articles that it quickly became apparent that a shortage of material would not be an obstacle to producing a collection. The problem would rather be what to leave out.

I reluctantly concluded that the sports columns I had written over 15 years for the *Daily Telegraph*, often on the backstage politics of sport, had to be excluded from consideration, even though they included a campaign to save school playing fields, of which I was proud (and for which I was praised by the Duke of Edinburgh), as well as commenting on issues and personalities in rugby, cricket, football and athletics between 1993 and 2008. The problem is that they mainly dealt with matters that cropped up during that week or month and soon became dated.

The same thing applied, more or less, to all the columns I have written every week for 13 years for the *Majorca Daily Bulletin*, in which I am encouraged to write about anything that takes my fancy. I have also excluded all the media columns I contributed for several years to the *Independent* and the *Evening Standard*.

Where possible, I have tried to avoid any overlap with material contained in my newspaper memoir, though towering figures such as David Astor and Tiny Rowland who, in their different ways, were a major influence on my career, were bound to reappear.

Many of the articles in the book relate to issues of press freedom and to leading media personalities of the past half-century; these have provided the main focus of my professional life. But as a newspaper editor I was also able to use my position, and my contacts, to gain access to famous figures — some serious, some not so serious — from other areas of life, both in Britain and abroad.

The articles are substantially as I wrote them at the time, though here and there I have cut some paragraphs or inserted a passage from another article I had written on the same subject or person. The earliest entries are from a sports magazine, *Light Blue*, which I helped to found at Cambridge, and from the *Sheffield Telegraph*, where I spent a couple of years as a graduate trainee before being posted to Africa in 1963 and then joining the *Observer* in London in 1966.

I am immensely grateful to the *Observer*, the *Sunday Times*, the *Guardian*, the *Daily Telegraph*, the *Independent*, the *Daily Mail*, the *Evening Standard*, the *Illustrated London News* and the *Sheffield Telegraph* for so readily agreeing to allow me to use material from their pages. I would also like to thank the Immediate Media Company for permission to reproduce some articles I wrote for the late lamented *Listener* magazine.

A powerful personal reason for producing this collection was that my two youngest children — Ben, aged nine, and Poppy, six — will discover in later life, after I have gone, what their old Dad had been up to in all those years before they were born.

I would also like to thank my agent, Jonathan Lloyd, and my publisher, Robert Hyde, for having faith in the project; Gina Hallam for slavishly inputting articles from the pre-digital era; and, as always, my wife Claire, my best critic, for her helpful advice on what, and what not to include, and for her patience when I was locked away for so many hours in my study. And I promise, finally, to get rid of all those files and boxes — well, most of them anyway.

Donald Trelford, February 2020

1 | EARLY DAYS

AN ALL-AMERICAN BOY

These reports, on ice hockey and tiddlywinks, appeared in Light Blue, *a sports magazine I set up at Cambridge with Alan Britten, nephew of Benjamin Britten.*

You would never have guessed it was a Varsity Match. The decayed Victorian grandeur of Richmond Sportsdrome seemed designed for gentler things. There was Victor Sylvester poised on the stage at one end of the rink, straining into the "Entry of the Gladiators" whenever he got the chance. There was a bar at the other end from which noises unrelated to the game would emerge from time to time. The spectators themselves were mostly leather-jacketed locals. There was even a display of figure skating to keep us all amused during the frequent breaks. It all made a pattern — only the players seemed out of place.

Perhaps that was because less then ten per cent of them were British. The Oxford side contained four Americans and ten Canadians — of whom ten were Rhodes scholars. Cambridge were rather more cosmopolitan, finding room for seven Canadians, three Americans, a Southern Rhodesian, a Brazilian, two Englishmen and a Scotsman.

To one whose knowledge of the game had hitherto been restricted to a dim awareness of the name of Chick Zamyck, it was all very confusing. But there was at least one familiar figure — "Two Gun Pete" Dawkins, pride of Brasenose and West Point, last seen galloping down the wing at Twickenham, now standing aloof in the centre of the rink, ruminatively chewing his gum like the good All-American boy he is. He had good reason to ruminate. Last year he broke a collar-bone in this very match.

There was a seemingly endless period of warming-up, during which one particularly thuggish Oxford yank seemed intent on knocking my pen from my hand — or worse. Then the game started, and inside a minute my thuggish friend was cooking his temper in the penalty box — a journey he was to repeat many times before the game was over.

The score at the end of the first period was 3-2 to Oxford, after M. Bradley (St. John's) and J. C. Taylor (Trinity Hall) had scored the first two goals for Cambridge. Oxford's second goal was ominous. Dawkins, who was billed as a full-back and who had been playing a sort of Johnny Haynes role in the centre of the rink, suddenly swooped on the puck, took a few predatory strides, and scored as if nobody else was there.

Cambridge fought their way back level during the second period, thanks chiefly to some fearless reflex saves by the goal-minder S. R.

Longley (Peterhouse), and two more goals by Taylor. In the next half period the score went from 4-4 to 5-5. Dawkins got his third for Oxford and J. G. Dearlove (Queens') replied with an opportunist crack. At this stage it looked like Dawkins v. Cambridge. Despite bewildering changes in personnel, Dawkins stayed on and on...and on. Cambridge seemed to be changing their variables rather more frequently. But in mounting excitement, Oxford gradually took the initiative.

It was still 5-5 with ten minutes to go, but Cambridge had their eyes on the clock. They defended bravely but Oxford, prompted by Dawkins, came through twice to score in powerful style. At the end they all rushed to acclaim Dawkins. But the All-American boy just kept on chewing.

MAKING TIDDLYWINK HISTORY

On February 18, 1961, under the gilded, pseudo-baroque ceiling of the Cambridge Masonic Hall, tiddlywink history was made. Oxford won the third Annual Inter-Varsity Tiddlywink match by 59 ½ points to 52 ½. But that was not all. It was the first defeat by Cambridge since the club was founded in 1954.

It was obvious before the match that this year's result would be no mere formality. Basic, irreconcilable differences in the attitudes of our two great universities had become apparent, indicated by the appearance of the two sides — Cambridge uniformly immaculate in white shirts and bow ties, Oxford uniformly scruffy in anything they could lay their hands on.

One difference related to women. Cambridge have always opposed their admittance to the club. This year's Oxford team contained three, which indicates something — possibly about the women. Another difference concerned the amount of time allowed per game.

Cambridge have always had a 20-minute rule, and have played directly for the pot, eschewing subtle defensive operations. Oxford have played without limit, thus allowing themselves time to develop the most intricate manoeuvres. Their favourite tactic is "double-squopping", a defensive ploy designed to render their opponents inactive. After animated discussion a 35-minute compromise was reached, but it was clear from the mood of icy politeness in which the match was conducted that both sides felt that they had been cheated.

"Squopping" involves landing on the opponents' winks, which are thereby neutralised. An opponent is forbidden to move when so covered. Cambridge, with a traditional emphasis on attack, encouraged only one of each pair to "squop", while the other set his sights directly on the pot. The Oxford pairs ignored the pot altogether at first, and concentrated instead on the negative task of putting the Cambridge pairs out of action. This was "double-squopping", and its effects were insidiously destructive.

It must not be thought that Cambridge surrendered their claim to the Duke of Edinburgh's Silver Wink without a fight. For two thirds of the match they were ahead, and in spite of television cameras squinting disconcertingly over their shoulders, Messrs. Furlonger, Bardsley, Woodhead and Clarke exhibited the slickest of winking fingers. But, as one authority put it, "double-squopping was finally vindicated."

Spike Milligan should have been there to umpire, but he couldn't make it, so the Rev. E.A. Willis, first secretary of the English Tiddlywinks Association, came along instead. As Mr Willis truly said in his presentation address: "This is a sad day for Cambridge." And it has to be admitted that the club has not yet completely thrown off the disappointment— even after a resounding victory over Joe Loss and his Orchestra at the Hammersmith Palais itself.

Light Blue, 1961

HOW THEY REMEMBER "BERT" LAWRENCE

I joined the Sheffield Telegraph *in 1961, the year after the obscenity trial over* Lady Chatterley's Lover. *As Lawrence was born within the newspaper's circulation area, I set off to find anyone who remembered him, 32 years after his death. I struck lucky.*

Eastwood is one of those small, untidy mining villages stuck on the edge of Erewash Valley, about a mile from the border between Nottinghamshire and Derbyshire. It is hilly country, looking west towards Matlock, 16 miles away, and north-east towards Mansfield and Sherwood Forest.

To D.H. Lawrence as a boy at the turn of the century it was still the England of the old agricultural past; there were no motor-cars; the mines were, in a sense, an accident on the landscape, and Robin Hood and his merry men did not seem far away.

That's how Lawrence described it later, to account for the love-hate relationship he always bore towards Eastwood. It seemed to him that there the old world and the new came together. What hurt him was the contrast between Eastwood as it stood and the beautiful hill-top village it might have been. That contrast remained a painful symbol to him throughout the rest of his life: "The country is so lovely: the man-made England so vile."

But the Lawrence country is still there for those who want to find it. The slate and brick of Eastwood itself; smoking Brinsley below; Greasley with its traces of castle; Beauvale's broken medieval walls and High Park Wood beyond; the sheet of water at the edge of the wood and the little valley between High Park and Willey Spring. At the end of his life Lawrence wrote: "That's the country of my heart."

His father was a butty at Brinsley Colliery with a reputation for cheeking his seniors. His grandfather had been a prize-fighter, and his mother's grandfather wrote some famous hymns.

He was born at Eastwood in 1885, the fourth child in a family of five, and died in France in 1930. The eldest brother, George, became a textile engineer and now lives at Bournemouth. Ernest, the second son, died at the age of 23.

★★★

In 1915 D.H. Lawrence wrote in a letter to his old friend Willie Hopkin: "Get me a few people in Sheffield, will you — people who care vitally about the freedom of the soul — a few people anywhere — but only those who really care." Willie Hopkin was the postman at Eastwood and fast bowler in the village cricket team, as well as a poet who wrote a column in the local paper every week until he died at the age of 90.

I don't know if Willie Hopkin actually found the people Lawrence wanted. But I do know that there are a number of people in Sheffield and the surrounding areas of Derbyshire and Nottinghamshire who met Lawrence in his lifetime and preserve first-hand recollections of him like faded family snapshots. I talked to some of them.

Denis is a businessman in Sheffield. He is 53 now, but when he was about 12 he lived at Eastwood and met him a number of times at semi-literary house-parties thrown by Willie Hopkin. His recollections of Lawrence are frankly unflattering. "I remember that admiring throng of ten to fifteen people around him, who obviously thought highly of him. They always talked about him and when they changed the subject he got very annoyed.

"He had no time for me at all. Of course, I was only a boy and he thought boys were very small fry indeed. He was so egotistical, he couldn't be bothered with children — at least, that was my impression.

"He couldn't be bothered with people who didn't worship him. He didn't impress me at all. I thought he was just a self-conscious egotist completely uninterested in any conversation that wasn't about him.

"He couldn't come off his pedestal and play marbles, you know. Everybody else played darts or billiards or cricket, but not Lawrence — he wouldn't join in and play anything. When that happened, he'd go off on his long walks through the country.

"I think that was his great failing as an individual, he wasn't able to see much into other people's lives. He had a one-track mind. You must remember that I was only a boy. Now I might have looked on him more tolerantly.

"It may not have been his fault either. Perhaps the other people there weren't worth bothering with."

★★★

Willie Hopkin's first wife, Sally, who came from Sheffield, died before Lawrence did, but his second wife, Betty, still lives at Eastwood in a house filled with memories of two remarkable men. She has a collection of first editions signed by Lawrence that makes the mouth water.

She showed me a picture of some flowers that Lawrence painted, and some of Lawrence's letters to her husband. In one of these he thanked Willie Hopkin for sending him "good old crusty Eastwood gossip."

"But Lawrence didn't like Eastwood, you know. He once said he'd be glad if it was puffed from the face of the earth. And Eastwood people don't think much of Lawrence either.

"My husband put a plaque over the house where Lawrence was born in Victoria Street, but nobody else has bothered at all. The older women remember how he put Flossie Cullen and her father in *The Lost Girl* and they've never really forgiven him. (The lost girl in question runs off with a passing Italian showman in Lawrence's story. In real life she married very respectably and settled down in Eastwood.)

"And the old miners think more of his father, who worked in Brinsley Colliery from the time he was seven and was a fine singer and the best dancer in the district.

"I met Lawrence for the first time at his sister Ada's at Ripley. She was a good friend of mine. It was a family gathering and I felt very strange, a bit out of it. Frieda, Lawrence's wife, was there. My husband used to say she was like a mountain breeze in the house. She was a very vivid personality. My stepdaughter Enid went out to New Mexico after Lawrence died in 1930 and helped Frieda sort out his letters and things.

"Frieda was never keen on cooking or anything like that. Lawrence was — he loved cooking and sewing. It must have been very difficult for her, a baroness, to marry an ordinary man with no money.

"Lawrence could get very angry. Frieda and he used to slang each other all the time, but it didn't mean anything. She used to call him Lorenzo or anything except his proper name. We called him Bert. Yes, always Bert.

"He had a red beard and was very striking. He was tallish and very slim – the women in Eastwood say he was the thinnest lad they ever saw. He had a broad nose — all the family have got that. He had no local accent at all, but he used to put it on sometimes with my husband for a laugh.

"Once, when Lawrence was about 14, he was with my husband in the kitchen. He suddenly said: 'Willie, I'm going to be an author.' My husband said he must be prepared to have his manuscripts returned a few times. Bert's face flushed slightly as he replied: "I have genius! I know I have!"

"When Bert was very young, my husband saw the village boys marching behind him shouting 'Dicky, Dicky Denches plays with the Wenches.' Of course, Lawrence did always go with the girls, but that was because he was too frail to play games.

"He liked the lively ones, though, and couldn't be bothered with the plain Janes. He was a lovely dancer, like his father. And he could be very witty. My husband told a tale about the time some girls came into a room and my husband stood up for them. Bert said: 'For goodness sake don't be polite. Let them find their own. When you get to Heaven you'll get up for every blessed woman who enters until the last seat is gone, and then you'll fall backwards into Hell — and serve you jolly well right.'

"Connie Chatterley? I once asked Bert who she was, and he told me. But I'm not telling you!"

★★★

Lawrence's sister, Ada, became Mrs Clarke and died at Ripley. The other sister, Emily, is 80 and lives in an isolated wooden bungalow just outside Newark. She is now confined to bed and was too ill to see me when I called, but her husband Samuel King, a spry man of 82, had a lot to say about the early days.

We talked first on the windy verandah of the bungalow and later stood with our backs to a roaring fire in the grate. "I knew Bert Lawrence when he was a very young lad with a snuffy nose, but we went to different schools and I lost sight of him. I was a few years older than he was, and never really got to know him until I married his sister.

"When their mother died in 1910, the family home was broken up and Bert came to live with us. Bert thought the world of his mother. Not long after that, he went to be a school-teacher — and he was a good one, whatever people like to think.

"I could tell you a lot that's never been told about those days, but it wouldn't do any good now. There's only one journalist we've ever spoken to before, so you're very lucky. They all came round last year when the Chatterley fuss was on, but I told them to clear off. Most of them had never read his books.

"Everybody knows about *Lady Chatterley's Lover* being banned and burnt and all that, and how his paintings were seized at that exhibition in London by the police for being obscene. Look at that picture on the wall — that was one of them in the exhibition. Nowt obscene about that, is there?" The picture he showed me was charming and quite inoffensive. It showed a naked little black girl serving at table.

"You know, Bert was a painter long before he was a writer. People don't always realise that. And I'll tell you something else they don't know either — about *Lady Chatterley's Lover*. I haven't told anybody before, it's only just come back to me.

"When I was a lad of eight my Dad was colliery manager at Brinsley, and I remember he came home one day with some scandal about a game-keeper on one of the big estates, and the daughter of the house. They tried to keep it from me, as I was just a slip of a lad, but it came back to me just recently. I don't know why I've never remembered it before.

"I can't tell you which estate it was on, and I haven't been able to puzzle out which of them it was. They all had a game-keeper's hut and a daughter of the house. "Bert Lawrence would still be in his pram at that time, but he must have got hold of the story later, and mixed it in with other stories, the way he always did.

"Mind you. I've kissed Lady C. myself you know. What do I mean? I mean I've kissed Frieda, that's who. When Lawrence stayed with us once, I asked him outright. I said: 'Bert, who is Connie Chatterley?' And he said: 'Why, she's mostly Frieda, of course.'

"Look here, we've got a first edition of *Lady Chatterley's Lover,* with an inscription from Lawrence to my wife. It's one of a thousand original copies. When my wife first read it, she said to him: "Bert, it's a wonderful book, but I wish you'd never written it.

"The last time Lawrence was in England he stayed with us at 16, Brooklands Road, Sneinton Hill, Nottingham. I remember we used to go for long walks. It was always exciting to go for a walk with Bert. He'd notice things you never knew were there. He had great respect for living things. He'd never harm a fly, he was so gentle. He'd tell you what it was like to be a bird or an animal and you'd think you were under its skin. He'd be very angry if anyone told smutty stories.

"To my wife he was always a simple, kind, loving brother. She went over to Switzerland to see him before he died. He was a fine a man as ever lived — you tell the people that. But they won't take any notice, you know."

It was Lawrence's other sister, Ada, who said: "One day he will come home to them in his books, and they will learn the truth about him and understand his life; and what is perhaps more important, they will learn a little truth about themselves."

Sheffield Telegraph, 1962

2 | FIFTY YEARS ON

A DINOSAUR DAD

The Sunday Times *asked me to write this article when our son Ben was born in 2011. Three years later, when I was 76, we had a daughter, Poppy. By an odd coincidence, my father was born in 1911 and my mother in 1914.*

It is 3am and a baby is crying in my arms. Rain is lashing at the window and a cat is scratching at the door. Come to think of it, the baby was also crying at 2am, and at 1am, come to that. The baby is Ben, now a month old, and his old man — his old, old man — is trying to keep him happy, or at least quiet, walking him around the bedroom in the dark. Having been sleepy all day, Ben tends to get rowdy at night — I wonder who he gets that from.

This reminds me of the reported reaction of friends at the Garrick Club when they read that I was to become a father again — as the club newsletter put it, "seven years before he joins our growing band of octogenarians". The stunned conversation in the bar evidently went like this: "But how's he going to cope with 3am feeds?" Silence all round as they stare glumly into their drinks, then one joker says: "As I recall, Donald used to be at his best around 3am."

They should see me now, though, stumbling around in a daze, eyes half-closed with the baby's head resting on a piece of muslin on my left shoulder in case of a mishap, that snail's trail on the jumper with which all fathers become sadly familiar.

As I do this, I have a strange sense of déjà vu, of other babies and other cries, in what seems like a lifetime ago. The nocturnal prowling with a cloth on the shoulder takes me back four (or is it five?) decades to similar rituals with my older children — Sally, now aged 46, Tim, 44, Paul, 41, and Laura, 30. The sudden arrival of a younger brother must have shocked them even more than it did me, though one of them was heard to mutter: "Nothing my father does surprises me any more."

I left the older ones when they were very young, and it would be understandable if they were to resent the love being poured on the *arriviste*. But my wife Claire and I were pleased and rather touched that two of my children, Sally and Paul, chose to fly out to Palma to see their young half-brother the day after he was born.

Paul said nothing had moved him so much as holding baby Ben since the birth of his own two boys. Laura immediately posted Ben's picture on her Facebook page. An ex-wife sent a greetings card. There are also four grandchildren, which causes generational confusion. My grandson

Freddie wrote a letter to his new uncle that began: "Dear Ben, I hope the birth went well."

I must have been about 10 years old, the same age as Freddie is now, when I did a morbid calculation, lying awake at night in my bedroom, as to how long I could expect to live. Having been born in 1937, I worked out by mental arithmetic that I would be coming up to 63 at the time of the millennium and reckoned that, given a slice of luck, I should be around for that landmark.

But when would I die? That was a more difficult equation. I remember clearly that I decided on 73 as a suitable age to pop my clogs. In those days I thought people of 35 were middle-aged, so to reach the age of 73 seemed an astonishing feat of longevity. What I didn't take into my calculations was that I would be having a child at 73.

When news of Claire's pregnancy came out in the summer, I was bombarded with requests from several newspapers to tell my story. What story? I asked. "Well," said one, "it's a chance to defend yourself." Defend myself? Why should I have to defend myself? Then I started reading about elderly fathers such as Michael Douglas, Elton John and Rod Stewart — all attacked, mainly by female columnists, for being too old to have children — and the recognition dawned that I am older than all of them.

I am, in fact, the same age as Charlie Chaplin was when his last child was born. He had run off with his wife Oona, daughter of the playwright Eugene O'Neill, when she was 18, and 36 years his junior. I am older than Julio Iglesias was when he had his last child (63) or Luciano Pavarotti (67) or Picasso (also 67). But not as old as Anthony Quinn (81) or a guy in India who recently claimed to have sired a child at 94.

My wife is 25 years younger than me, which hasn't been a problem for either of us. This is Claire's first marriage and her first child. That is why I don't feel any need to defend the fact that, despite my age, we have had this baby together. Claire decided she wanted a child when it was almost too late for her to have one. Obviously it would have been better to have had one earlier in our 14-year relationship, since I would have been that much younger and would live to see more of the child growing up. But it didn't happen. Anyone who says I shouldn't be having a child at my age is saying that Claire should not have a child at all, which I don't believe anyone is entitled to say about another human being.

When we met in 1997, Claire was a television producer and

presenter and had worked for Sky and the BBC. Her family had had a holiday home in Mallorca since she was a child and we started coming here regularly. Eventually we bought a place of our own and moved out in 2003, having married two years before.

We live in a converted finca on the side of a mountain, a 10-minute walk from the old town of Pollença, with a big garden and grounds, including an orchard of fruit trees and plenty of hideaways where a boy can play. Before Ben came along, we had often said it was a perfect place for a child to grow up.

Health and safety factors will need to be addressed, with a pool and some steep drops in need of fencing off. We had a new path laid down just over a year ago on a slope in the front garden. When the builder was working out the right size for the paving stones, he asked, tongue in cheek: "Should I be planning for a pushchair or a wheelchair?" I replied: "It may be touch and go." Fortunately, the pushchair came first.

When a former colleague heard about the impending birth, he exploded: "It was an accident, wasn't it? You can't have deliberately planned for a life of nappies and buckets and spades at your age, Donald — surely!" Ben wasn't an accident. He was the result of many years of trying, first in London, then, successfully, in Spain. The London experience of fertility treatment was dispiriting. We were made to feel pessimistic about the outcome at every stage and didn't feel that the medical staff really cared one way or the other.

In Spain it was the opposite. They were optimistic from the start, made us feel optimistic, and were genuinely thrilled when it worked. But then the Spanish, especially Mallorquins and especially the men, are notoriously sentimental about babies. We are stopped all the time in the street by people wanting to pick Ben up, calling him "*guapo*" (handsome) or "*bonito*" (pretty) — which, of course, he is.

Friends assumed that Claire would have the baby in England, but we decided to remain on the island. My age never seemed to be a problem from a medical point of view; the doctors were more concerned that Claire's age (48) made her old to be expecting a first child. Given our ages, more than 120 combined, we were naturally concerned that the child could be born with abnormalities, but we were soon reassured by the ultra-modern scanning technology, which had advanced beyond belief since I last accompanied a pregnant wife to a hospital. The images were blown up enormously.

On one occasion I was standing in front of the screen with my glasses on the end of my nose, earnestly trying to identify the facial features. I was sure I had just identified a nose and a chin when the doctor chipped in: "That's his kidneys."

"How can you cope at your age?" is the question people are too polite to ask. The truth is that, in many ways, I am better equipped to cope than I was with my older children. Then I was deeply immersed in my career, editing a paper in Malawi then climbing the executive ladder at the *Observer*, working all hours. Now my wife and I can spend our time at home together, concentrating on the baby.

Even when I am writing, I am just next door in my study and can be summoned in a moment for the parental duties we share. Claire does breast, I do bottle. In fact, I am in charge of BBC: bottles, burps and changing nappies. I know it's still early days, but I am enjoying it all immensely, though the 24/7 attention span is rather daunting. Getting the pushchair up and down and fixing the car seat still challenge my technical skills and I have learnt not to wear my glasses on a string round my neck (though there is little time for reading books at the moment anyway).

My beard is a source of fascination, though it hasn't yet provoked the reaction it did in my grandson Ollie, who told his parents in a profoundly serious voice: "Grandad has a beard just like God!" As for getting up at night, it's a definite advantage that older people need less sleep and usually make one or two nocturnal loo trips anyway, though one can't help being mildly irritated to wake up knackered and find that the cause of your fatigue is bright-eyed and raring to go.

A baby is a joy, an affirmation of life, a cause for celebration, and in our case a bit of a miracle. I know that it is right, whatever carping columnists may say, that we should have had Ben, even if he is destined not to have the very long relationship with his father that I enjoyed with mine — 64 years. But that was exceptional and many children lose a parent in early life and go on to lead happy and successful lives. A friend of mine died months before his daughter was born.

Besides, what matters in a relationship is its quality; Ben will have my full attention which, to my regret, my older children never had. All my children made me proud, but having children then, nearly half a century ago, was a different experience for a man. I know things have changed since then and fathers now have an acknowledged central role in child-rearing, but then it was, roughly speaking, something wives got on with while a man got on with his job. That sounds crude, but I'm afraid it was largely true.

With Ben it feels completely different, chiefly because I have so much time for him. As I push him along the beautiful Pine Walk in Puerto Pollença, with the winter sun glinting off the sea, the boats and the mountains across the bay, I feel a sense of wellbeing and contentment that I have rarely known before. The other day, while I was waiting for my wife, I stopped off at a posh hotel on the front and pushed Ben into the lounge. He started crying when the pushchair came to a halt, so I took out a bottle and started to feed him, rather self-consciously in those plush surroundings.

I needn't have worried. The Spanish waiters all came over to coo. They were joined by a group of well-spoken English blue-rinse widows in their finery, holding G&Ts, oozing class and privilege. Ben took one look at them all and let fire the biggest burp — a real Sir Toby of a belch — that I have ever heard outside a rugby changing room. I choose to interpret this as his first act of social defiance. That's my boy!

The *Sunday Times*, 2011

3 | OBSERVATIONS

ANCESTRAL VOICES

Lewis Doxat, the first known editor of the *Observer,* used to pride himself on never writing 'an article on any subject under any circumstances whatever.' But he was the first to understand the power and profit of advertising. He arrived in England from the West Indies and died at the age of 108. If he could know that the *Observer* of 1791 had survived for 10,000 editions — and was the only Sunday paper of its time to come through — even he might permit an exception.

The anniversary provides an opportunity to hark back to what Paul Johnson recently described as a newspaper's 'ancestral voices,' through which its traditions speak and from which its personality derives. An editor ignores these voices at his peril, though he should not allow them to haunt him. In the *Observer's* case, what do the voices say?

The first issue proudly proclaimed itself "a vehicle of rational amusement...that cannot fail of becoming a favourite family paper ...whilst it breathes, invariably, towards all, the Spirit of enlightened Freedom, decent Toleration, and Universal Benevolence." It also contained a staggering obscenity based on the easy transposition of the 18th century "f" and "s." The founder, W.S. Bourne, went bust after three years and tried to sell it to the government.

How it alone survived of the many Sunday newspapers on sale at the time is a mystery. The clue probably lies in the talents of W.I. Clement, whose innovations included the crime story and the first woodcut engravings in the British press, He also understood that what sells newspapers is news.

Wellington, with whom the paper was in frequent dispute over reform, was among the first of many public men who have looked in vain for that promised "Toleration and Universal Benevolence." Pitt, and later Palmerston and Melbourne, secured the paper's support in the time-honoured way — by paying for it. Palmerston had a Secret Service fund which assured him of a good press; he even wrote *Observer* editorials backing his own policies. Most newspapers at this time took money from the Government, or from political parties, in return for publicising speeches.

The *Observer's* Vincent Dowling, the hottest reporter of his time — who not only witnessed the murder of the Prime Minister, Spencer Perceval, in the House of Commons in 1812, but apprehended the killer — moonlighted as a Home Office spy. The *Observer* took its last recorded bribe in 1840.

Newspapers pocketed the money because it was the only way to survive. Governments of the time, anxious to suppress dissent in the wake of the French Revolution, stacked the odds against new publications with the infamous stamp duty (Cobden's "tax on knowledge"), an advertisement levy and an excise on paper. It was only when these taxes were abolished in the 1850s that newspapers could honestly claim a degree of independence. Instead, they became dependent on the market.

Sunday papers are a British phenomenon. They came into being because publishers could not afford the impost of dailies and because many readers could only afford the money and leisure for a weekly purchase. From the beginning, they were always more popular than dailies.

Because they started in a period of political upheaval, the Sunday papers have always had a sparky, more radical edge than the dailies. There was an irreverent, anti-Sabbatarian flavour about their very publication; they were forbidden fruit, sold in clubs, public houses and barbers' shops. Recalling the earlier chap-books and ballads, they had spicy stories about murders and elopements.

Dowling led Fleet Street with his coverage of Queen Caroline's notorious trial and divorce. (I'm glad to say that we took her side.) He went to France to get her story and rowed back to England with the scoop of the century on a journey that took 12 hours. The story turned public opinion in favour of the Queen and against King George IV. Perhaps because of this, the *Observer* was described in 1820 as "one of the safest of contemporary papers to be put into the hands of ladies."

Another early scoop was the paper's exposure of the Cato Street conspiracy of 1820, an attempt to blow up the entire British Cabinet. Incredibly, the Lord Chief Justice ordered the Press not to cover the trial, an order that was challenged and then ignored by the *Observer*, which thereby secured an important victory for freedom of reporting.

The success of the early *Observer* was such that a publisher of the time, Henry White, tried to steal its readers with a paper called *The Independent Observer*, later *The New Observer*. In 1822 he gave up and re-named it the *Sunday Times*.

But it wasn't only for news that the *Observer* acquired its reputation. Under the great nineteenth-century editors, Dicey and Traill, it was followed for its political intelligence, for its coverage of arts and books, and for its opinions on the issues of the day (many of which, when you look back through the files, turn out to be the issues of our own day too: political reform, education, poverty, Afghanistan, the threat from Russia to the Poles — and always, Ireland).

The paper started staunchly Tory, then supported the Whig reforms, and by 1880 was said to be "well-known to be in the confidence of sundry prominent personages amongst the Liberals." It bravely and unfashionably backed the North against the South in the American civil war ("Negro slavery is the blot upon North America"), took a surprising anti-colonial line at the time of the Indian Mutiny, and opposed Queen Victoria's elevation to Empress of India ("As well might our Queen be designated Sultana").

In the 1890s the two papers were to share an owner called Julius Beer. For a time his daughter-in-law Rachel Beer, who was Siegfried Sassoon's aunt, managed to edit both our great Sundays at once. She caused polite amusement by requiring letters to the editor to be prefixed "Dear Madam." Her greatest scoop was to establish the innocence of the French Jewish officer, Captain Dreyfus, by publishing the confession of Major Charles Esterhazy that he had forged the documents that incriminated Dreyfus and led to his incarceration on Devil's Island. In later life Rachel Beer was confined by her family for reasons of mental health.

If it is hard to discern a pattern in all this, the present century is no more helpful. Over 3,000 *Observers* — nearly a third of its total history — were edited by two very different personalities, J.L. Garvin and David Astor: the one rhetorical, dogmatic, pontifical ("Garvin was Lear," said his daughter when he died), the other questioning, quixotic and seemingly diffident (more of a Hamlet?).

Garvin, a maverick Tory, wrote a Johnsonian article of many thousands of words every week for 34 years. It came to dominate the *Observer* — Beachcomber wrote of readers spending whole Sundays "grazing on the lower slopes of Mount Garvin". Even though he rarely came to the office, dispatching his article by Rolls-Royce and train from Beaconsfield, Garvin gave the *Observer* unrivalled political authority before and after the First World War. His article on the Versailles Treaty of 1919 shows why: "The Treaty scatters dragons' teeth across the soil of Europe. They will spring up as armed men unless the mischief is eradicated by other and better labours."

David Astor, whose family originally bought the *Observer* from Northcliffe in 1911, made it a liberal, non-party newspaper after the Second World War, and directed readers' attention to the new problems of the post-war world — the end of colonialism in Africa, Asia and the Middle East and the need for peaceful co-existence through a global balance of power. Some notable scoops of this time came from reporting Communist countries seriously: Tito's split with Moscow, the Sino-Soviet split, the full text of Khrushchev's historic break with Stalinism, the memoirs of Stalin's daughter, Svetlana, and the truth about Kim Philby's defection (one of our less distinguished old boys).

At home the Astor *Observer* campaigned for liberalisation of the laws on divorce, censorship, homosexuality, abortion, for an end to capital punishment, for prison reform and (especially) racial toleration. In general, it encouraged the country's search for a society more in keeping with post-imperial realities. His stand at Suez ("We had not realised that our Government was capable of such folly and such crookedness") lost the paper some Jewish advertisers, but gained it lasting respect. Astor had a sharp eye for editorial talent. He widened the paper's appeal with a review section and a colour magazine, and before he retired in 1975 he had trebled Garvin's circulation.

In the 1980s, during my editorship, the *Observer* was accused of being "out of touch" with the current of right-wing thought and had suffered for this commercially. We were not "out of touch" with it: we opposed it and we suffered for our opposition, just as the paper suffered for being right over Suez three decades before. As Iain Macleod, the Conservative Chancellor, said to David Astor about that episode: "You can be wrong by being right too soon."

What of the next 10,000 *Observers*? As in any business, survival in Fleet Street depends on keeping costs below revenue, no easy task (and beyond the power of mere editors). In recent years, without generous support from Atlantic Richfield and now Lonhro, we would have found it hard to reach today's landmark. In the longer term the challenge is to attract new readers and retain the loyalty of old ones, since readers are finally the only source of a newspaper's strength.

What continuity does all this have with a paper founded for another age, in the year of Mozart's "Magic Flute?" Can an inner consistency be detected? We like to think so.

Part of the consistency is trying to look at things anew and not being a slave to what was said before, even by us; trying not to "con" readers that problems have easy solutions, and that we know what they are; being reasonable even if we can't always be right; giving off a strong whiff of idealism that attracts some people and irritates others; trying harder than some to be open-minded; not recoiling from the awkward truth when we see it; being, in Orwell's phrase (himself an *Observer* writer) the "enemies of nonsense," especially our own.

If this sometimes makes for what Conor Cruise O'Brien has called "muzziness, our besetting sin," one can only say that there are worse faults for a newspaper to have, like being untruthful, prejudiced or boring, which we hope we are not — except, perhaps, when we go on too long about ourselves.

The *Observer,* 1983

A GREAT EDITOR

This is the address I gave at the memorial service for David Astor at St Bride's Church, Fleet Street, in February 2002. He had died in December 2001, aged 89. He edited the Observer *from 1948 to 1993.*

D avid Astor was a great editor because he was a great man. The two things do not always go together. There are highly successful editors who are not great men — and, if the truth be told, are not always very good men either. In David, the man and the journalist were of a piece. If the *Observer* stood for important values and convictions, these came from him, dug painfully out from his own mind, heart and conscience. If the paper was characterised by humour, idealism, a sense of justice and a wide-ranging curiosity about the world and the vagaries of human nature — which it was — those qualities had their source in David's own complex and elusive personality.

Anyone talking about David in this way is troubled by the thought as to how he would react to hearing it — how he would raise a quizzical eyebrow and lower that fine head in embarrassment, for he was the most modest of men. I can just hear him now, uttering that phrase he used when he didn't want something to appear in the paper: "I'm a shade nervous about this". Approval he would express by saying "Okey-dokey" and, if you were very lucky, by giving you one of the peppermints he kept in his office.

It is sometimes thought that the chief requirement in an editor is decisiveness and certainty of judgement. David, as anyone who worked with him knows, sometimes belied that belief — so much so that the phrase, "the editor's indecision is final", was actually coined about him. This was not the case over major issues like Suez or apartheid, where he saw the truth with a blazing moral clarity. But over lesser decisions he frequently tortured himself — and, it has to be said, tortured his subordinates too (I can still see our great managing editor, Ken Obank, and the head printer wringing their hands in agony outside David's office as he wrestled with a final page proof).

This hesitation was caused by two things, I believe. A kind of perfectionism rare in newspapers, a determination to say the right thing — above all, to avoid saying the wrong thing — no matter how long it might take, because he believed that it matters what newspapers say and that they have a duty to be fair to people in public life — a result, I think, of the unkind way in which the press had sometimes treated his mother.

It was also because he didn't like laying down the law. He operated in an oblique, rather feline way, prompting people towards a solution rather than imposing it on them. But that hesitant manner of his, the apparent diffidence, masked a steely determination. One of my senior colleagues said to me:"In all the time I've known David, I never once heard him raise his voice".There are few, if any, other editors of whom that can be said. Or people for that matter.

David's *Observer* was also rare among newspapers in that it made no claim to omniscience. There were no thumping certitudes on every subject under the sun. I once heard him say:"There are some problems in this life to which there are no answers.There are other problems to which there may be answers, but we don't happen to know what they are".This attitude gave special authority to the paper's opinions when it did express them.

If David were to hear this address, I can anticipate one of his objections. He would say:"It wasn't just me, you know — there were many others."And that, of course, is true — though it was David who selected them and the sheer resonance of the names of the writers and thinkers he gathered around him is evidence of David's brilliance in an editor's most important skill — as a talent-spotter : George Orwell, Arthur Koestler, Alistair Buchan, Sebastian Haffner, E.F. Schumacher, Philip Toynbee, Kenneth Tynan, Edward Crankshaw, Patrick O'Donovan, Katharine Whitehorn, Gavin Young, Neal Ascherson, Michael Frayn, Hugh McIlvanney, among many, many others.

None of these were orthodox journalists and David did not find them in an orthodox way. He recruited Nigel Gosling, an old school friend who became a distinguished art critic, at a bus stop. Terry Kilmartin, who became a great literary editor without ever going to university, had served with David in SOE during the war. Clifford Makins, a brilliant though rather shambolic sports editor, was plucked from the *Eagle*, a children's comic. Michael Davie was offered the job of diplomatic correspondent while still an Oxford undergraduate, on the strength of some letters he had written about his holidays. Sadly for journalism, that couldn't happen today.

David always insisted that nobody was too important, or too unimportant, to write for a newspaper. He was always rather suspicious of so-called professional journalists, whom he referred to as "plumbers": for him, a journalist should be someone who had something to say or who wanted something done in the world. I was asked by a colleague in my early days on the paper: "Are you a plumber or a journalist?" What's the difference? I asked, rather puzzled. "Well", said John Silverlight: "Are you here to help David save the *Observer* or to help him save the world?" "A bit of both, I hope," I muttered unconvincingly.

David used to liken running a newspaper to being the conductor of an orchestra. Others have likened it to running a theatre, which of course David did in the North of England before the war. He had a habit of wearing his coat across his shoulders like a cloak, in a way described by John Heilpern as that of an actor-manager. However, given the wild and eccentric figures he collected on the *Observer*, a more apt description might be a circus-master, with slow-moving elephants and a cage of naughty monkeys.

Like many people, I owe a great deal in my life to David. Before I ever knew him, I was educated by the *Observer* as a teenager in the 1950s, as were many people of my generation. It gave us a political and moral education that no school or university could provide. Colin Legum introduced us to Africa, Cyril Dunn to India, Dennis Bloodworth to China and the Far East, Robert Stephens and Patrick Seale to the Middle East, Anthony Sampson to the mysterious workings of the British Establishment. Christopher Brasher and Michael Davie showed that sport could be written about with the same style and intelligence as politics or the arts.

The *Observer* taught several generations in the post-war world how to think and feel about the great issues affecting Britain and the wider world. It became part of our conscience. David was at the heart of this process, not because he had a political programme to deliver — he didn't fit into any party moulds — but because he puzzled things out for himself and, in so doing, helped others to think for themselves, unencumbered by class or ideology.

It was the war, of course, that forced him to do this. I think he saw the problems of this island with a greater clarity because he was partly American. It also helped that, as a child at Cliveden, he had mixed with the leading figures of the day and was underawed by those set above us. I remember hearing him put a Prime Minister gently in his place when he tried to bully him into sacking Nora Beloff.

David's philosophy — inasfar as he had one — began with people and their suffering and how it should be relieved. It grew out of his natural kindness. As his great friend Sam Beer once said, "I have never known anyone who cared so much about being kind, from rescuing a donkey from a bad master to helping battered women to financing anti-apartheid efforts". And, as Anthony Sampson pointed out, even David's initials, FDLA, sounded like a freedom movement.

If I had to choose one word to describe David, I'd say "quixotic." Of the many things I owe him, apart of course from entrusting me with the continuation of his life's work on the *Observer*, was the conviction he passed on that the simple questions in life are the most important, the most interesting and the most difficult — and that the job of a newspaper is to go on asking them.

David taught me many things about editing, including the important principle that the paper should always be better than the editor. By this he meant that an editor who acted like a dictator and banned any opinions he didn't agree with, and removed staff who disagreed with him, could only produce a paper as good as himself. David insisted that the paper should always be better than that.

As a result, he took risks — with people and with ideas — insisting only that they be "authentic," one of his favourite words. Another word that always amused him was "sound", as in the civil service phrase, "Is he sound?" David used to say: "If he's sound, he's no use to me".

Through his many years on the *Observer* and in his myriad other activities — many of which we on the paper never knew about — David affected so many people's lives and changed so many things for the better that the tentacles of his goodness and achievements will go on reaching out long after him. His great friend Gustaw Gottesman, the Polish editor and intellectual, once wrote with David in mind: "Some people, like old oaks or elms, do not die. They just go on, stretching their arms for something which is eternal and indefinable, the real meaning of life".

St Bride's Church, 2002

The patter of Tiny's feet

It began in the parched earth of Matabeleland, among the cactus and the baobab trees, and ended over lunch in a Park Lane casino, served by long-legged girls in fishnet tights. For two hectic weeks the battle was monitored in every news bulletin, causing anguished debates in Parliament and the media about press freedom — and almost led to the the *Observer* being sold to Robert Maxwell.

The public row between me, as Editor of the *Observer*, and Tiny Rowland, then Chief Executive of Lonrho, the international conglomerate which had bought the newspaper three years before, grew into a Fleet Street soap opera that overshadowed the tragic human story that provoked it — the suffering of the minority Ndebele people at the hands of the North Korean-trained Fifth Brigade of the Zimbabwe Army.

I went to interview Robert Mugabe, the Zimbabwean Prime Minister, in April 1984 for a current affairs series on Channel 4 to mark the fourth anniversary of the country's independence. I also planned to write a piece for the the *Observer*, though the paper was not paying my expenses; I told Rowland about the visit as a courtesy, since his company had started in the former Rhodesia (hence "Lonrho") and had major business interests there.

That was a mistake, since it gave Rowland an opportunity to ingratiate himself with Mugabe ("I have arranged for my editor to publish an interview in the *Observer*") and try to repair relations that had been damaged by Lonrho's long support for the opposition leader, Joshua Nkomo.

When I arrived in Harare, I was met by Rowland's Zimbabwe "fixer", Godwin Matatu, who whisked me off for lunch with Lonrho's local board. The interview was clearly to be a Lonrho production and Matatu, a gregarious, alcoholic journalist, was to be my minder.

The Mugabe interview was disastrously dull, unusable for television, of interest only to a specialist African magazine (where, in fact, it subsequently appeared). When I asked him if he would consider a political rather than a military solution in Matabeleland, where a curfew had been in force since February, he replied bluntly: "The solution is a military one. Their grievances are unfounded. The verdict of the voters was cast in 1980. They should have accepted defeat then." He added chillingly: "The situation in Matabeleland is one that requires change. The people must be reoriented."

After I had appeared as guest of the week on ZBC, I was recognised by a group of Africans in the lobby of Meikles Hotel. One took me aside conspiratorially: "You should go to Matabeleland to see what is happening to our people there. There are terrible things. Go to the Hilton Hotel in Bulawayo, where we will find you." He hurried away, as if afraid to be overheard.

No media had been allowed inside the curfew area for 10 weeks, but there were rumours about brutal treatment of the population by Mugabe's soldiers, ostensibly searching for "dissidents" from across the Botswana border. I said to Matatu: "Let's go to Bulawayo in the morning."

We found little sign there of military activity, just the odd "hippo" armoured personnel carrier trundling along a dirt road with mounted guns, or a truck-load of troops with rocket-propelled grenades on their AK-47 rifles. Rain had made the Lowveld roads almost unpassable.

Schoolgirls were marching quietly in green check dresses or lying in the shade; old men scratching with hoes; cattle standing in the dry river beds, goats, donkeys, marmosets, even a kudu bull, dashing across the road.

We knew we weren't allowed officially into the curfew area, but asked our driver to brave the roadblocks anyway. We passed three without bother, all manned cheerily by policemen in brown boots, then Matatu did some name-dropping to persuade a tough-looking soldier to let us through. We were able to drive through the no-go areas, past Kezi, Antelope Mine, Bhalagwe Camp — all names, I learned later, that filled the Ndebele with dread, We saw nothing unusual.

Around 10pm, there was a call from the hotel reception in Bulawayo to say that a man wanted to deliver a letter. An African tapped on my door and handed it over. It read simply: "Please accompany this friend." Moving quietly to avoid disturbing Matatu next door. I followed the man to the car park, where a headlight beamed in recognition.

I had no idea where I was going, or with whom, and nobody knew where I'd gone. I knew instinctively that I couldn't take Matatu with me. Apart from the Lonrho connection, he was a Shona and close to the government and his presence would have deterred people from speaking honestly.

I climbed nervously into the car and was taken in silence for several miles out of town into the curfew area. There — after a semi-comic interlude in which we gave a lift to a policeman — we stopped at a remote house, pipped horns for ages, and finally changed cars with another man.

He took us for another long ride to a religious mission where, for much of the night, I was given a series of eyewitness accounts, sworn affidavits and signed statements from victims of the Matabeleland atrocities. These were graphic, horrific and profoundly moving.

One name kept recurring, as in a nightmare. Brigadier Shiri, known as Black Jesus, was head of the Fifth Brigade. And there was one recurring story, about a major who held up a dead baby and told villagers: "This is what will happen to your babies if you help dissidents." He then dropped the tiny corpse in the dust.

Back in the car again, I met a man from Esigodoni village who had been beaten close to death by agents of the Central Intelligence Organisation (CIO) in front of his family. They were warned they would be shot if they uttered a sound. "They began beating us with sticks and guns, bayoneting us, burning plastic against our skin while our hands and mouths were secured. They tore curtains, put cushions into our mouth. We were tortured for about four hours."

A man called Jason was brought to the house. He had been chopping trees at Welonke when two soldiers turned up with fixed bayonets and whips on their belt. They asked if he and his wife had seen any dissidents and grew increasingly angry when they said they hadn't. They beat his wife and grandmother and took him away.

Neighbours were collected and they all marched on, their progress broken by periodic beatings and a fight they were forced to stage for the soldiers' entertainment. At the village school they shot two children who had tried to run away. Eventually nine of them were forced to dig a hole to a depth of two or three feet and ordered to jump into it.

Jason told me: "The commander leaned against a tree, opened his radio cassette and shot five men. On the grave we put branches. I also saw a big grave which had stones on it. There are 16 buried in this grave."

Earlier I had come across Peter Godwin, of the *Sunday Times*, who said bodies had been thrown down a nearby mineshaft owned by Lonrho. (Later, Roy Hattersley was sued by Rowland for making this claim in a speech — what Rowland never knew was that I had helped to draft Hattersley's speech.)

Godwin had already got some atrocity stories into print, but he was inhibited by the fact that he couldn't betray his presence in the curfew area for fear of being expelled or, as a Zimbabwean himself, suffering even worse retribution. He had previously fought for Ian Smith's army against Mugabe's troops. Once he understood that I hadn't been sent by Rowland to put a Mugabe spin on the situation, we exchanged useful information.

I returned to the hotel at dawn, checked out without waking Matatu, then flew to London via Harare, arriving on Saturday morning with my story written. While in Harare I had two conversations. One was with a military attaché at the British High Commission, who wasn't at all surprised by the news from Matabeleland.

The other was with a South African director of Lonrho, Nick Kruger, who wasn't surprised either. "What you have discovered, Donald," he said, "is the eternal truth of Africa, Stuff them, then they stuff you. For centuries we stuffed the blacks; now it's their turn to stuff us. The Ndebele stuffed the Shona; now it's the Shona's turn."

My dilemma on returning — should I publish an anodyne interview with Mugabe or tell the truth about Matabeleland, thereby damaging the interests of my proprietor? — has since been written up as a classic case by the Institute of Global Ethics. For me, there was no choice.

I decided to ring Tiny around 5pm on Saturday, too late for him to do anything to stop publication, but before he could hear the news from anyone else. He slammed the telephone down after threatening the direst revenge.

Next morning I turned on the BBC eight o'clock news to hear my story condemned as lies in an official statement by Mugabe, supported by a letter of apology from Rowland. "I take full responsibility for what in my view was discourteous, disingenuous and wrong in the editor of a serious newspaper widely read in Africa." He described me as "an incompetent reporter" and announced that I would be dismissed.

I went ahead with a planned holiday to Guernsey, but quickly returned on the advice of Lord Goodman, the former *Observer* chairman, who said I must be seen on the bridge of my ship. The story was front-page news for a fortnight, "the most entertaining hullabaloo", as one writer put it, "since Harry Evans fell out with Rupert Murdoch".

Rowland wrote me an open letter, which he distributed to all papers before I could see it, saying Lonrho would not go on supporting a failing editor who showed no concern for their commercial interests. I replied in kind, pointing out that the circulation had actually gone up by 22 per cent in the eight years I had been editor. The *Daily Mail* published both letters in full under the headlines "Dear Donald" and "Dear Tiny".

Rowland insisted that I should go back to Zimbabwe for a longer investigation. I refused on the grounds that I had already established the truth of my story and that to do so would endanger the lives of my sources.

The Foreign Office, more concerned about relations with Mugabe than with human rights and doubtless sensitive that Britain had provided some training for the Fifth Brigade, was briefing against me. I learnt this from Prince Charles, with whom I happened to have lunch at that time. "The Foreign Office tell me you were wrong about Matabeleland," he said airily. I ate my soup in silence.

Paul Johnson in the *Spectator* said editors had no business trying to be reporters. John Junor wrote in the *Sunday Express*: "If Mr Trelford truly feels that way about Mr Rowland, wouldn't it be more honourable for him to stop accepting Mr Rowland's money?" The *Times* suggested I had forced a showdown deliberately. The *Daily Telegraph* said: "Those who pay the piper must be expected to demand some influence over the choice of tunes he plays."

The *Guardian* said the paper should "find its salvation where the people who write the cheques and the people who write the words can work together." This proved difficult at the *Observer* when Lonrho announced it was withdrawing financial support. Provoked by a ruling from the paper's independent directors that Rowland had interfered improperly, it put a hard-faced accountant in the office to stop me spending money.

This brought questions in Parliament. When Peter Shore for Labour asked Norman Tebbit what he planned to do to protect the editorial independence of the Editor of the *Observer* , the Secretary for Trade and Industry clearly enjoyed saying "Nothing". This was soon after the paper's revelations about Mark Thatcher's business connections with Oman.

The *Observer's* journalists were highly supportive of their editor — until Rowland let it be known he was planning to sell the paper to Maxwell. A meeting at Claridge's was announced for the next day. I knew Rowland would never sell to Maxwell and this was just a bluff to frighten the journalists. If so, it certainly worked.

I was interested in an interview with Maxwell about the *Observer*, which I heard on my car radio. He "greatly admired" me, he said, and would retain me as editor (which I seriously doubted). Then, asked what he would have done about the Mark Thatcher stories, he paused and replied in his deepest tone: "I'd have stamped on him." Whether he meant he would stamp on me or Mark Thatcher was unclear.

By now I felt the paper was being damaged and something had to be done to break the deadlock. So I wrote to Rowland offering my resignation: "I could not allow the paper's future and the prospects of its staff to be jeopardised by my personal position, which sadly seems to be all that stands in the way of the paper's development."

Rowland seized the olive branch and we made up over an edgy lunch in the incongruous ambience of one of Lonrho's London casinos. Undeterred by the pop music and scantily dressed females, we concocted a priceless statement that we shared an affection for three things — for Africa, for the *Observer*, and for each other.

For us and for the paper, that was the end of a remarkable and in some ways entertaining episode. For the people of Matabeleland, however, it provided only brief illumination before the darkness came again.

The *Observer*, 2000

4 | ODDBALLS

Mr Khashoggi's day in court

I attended the trial in New York of Adnan Khashoggi, the Saudi arms trader, and Imelda Marcos on fraud charges, of which they were acquitted. Khashoggi arranged for me to interview Mrs Marcos on his private jet (see Ten Miles High with Imelda*).*

At ten to nine every morning, a small family group— father, mother, son — emerges from the Olympic Tower on a corner of New York's Fifth Avenue, ignores the 5.7 litre silver stretch-Cadillac waiting at the kerb, and sets off on foot in the rain.

As St Patrick's Cathedral strikes nine, they pass the Waldorf Tower, where four men, waiting under umbrellas, fall into step behind them. They follow the same routine four days a week and are likely to go on doing so until the pavements burn under their feet in the summer.

At Lexington Avenue they queue for subway tokens, then change at Grand Central for the Downtown Express and jostle for space among the strap-hanging commuters — one of whom, I note, is reading St Augustine's *City of God*.

As they file out of Brooklyn Bridge station a raucous voice yells from the crowd: "You're going to rot in hell, Khashoggi!" The little man with the Poirot moustache half-turns; his eyes, as bright as ever behind unfamiliar spectacles, flash serious doubt about this prediction.

"Baba", cries his Italian wife Lamia, taking his arm as he stumbles on the station steps, and guides him across the road to the District Court of Lower Manhattan. It seems no time at all since "Baba" or A.K., as everyone else calls him, was plausibly described as "the richest man on earth".

Meanwhile, in the group ahead, a familiar coiffure is bobbing among the crowd. Imelda Marcos, former First Lady of the Philippines, is being steered past the boom mikes and cameras by a tall, silver-haired dude in a Stetson. She is joining Adnan Khashoggi in the dock as the least likely double-act in America's latest soap opera.

Still, at 60, an erect and surprisingly tall figure in widow's black, she too is halted by a hostile voice in the crowd. She turns, looking hunted and afraid. One recalls that she was once stabbed in a failed assassination bid in the Philippines. Later when I talk to her, I notice a tear-stain down one cheek, but it's no serious threat to her make-up.

The man in the Stetson is her lawyer, Gerry Spence from Wyoming, famous for his victory for Karen Silkwood (played in the film by Meryl

Streep). He was brought in late on the case when Imelda smartened up her act after the preliminary hearing: out went her previous counsel and an imperious royal blue ball gown which had reminded one unkind observer of Shea Stadium.

Khashoggi's team of lawyers, the men at the Waldorf Tower, have been with him for a year now, ever since he was dramatically snatched at the Schweitzerhof in Berne and extradited to the United States after three months in a Swiss jail. He spent eight days in the Manhattan Correction Centre before bail of $10 million was arranged. He still has to report to his local police precinct.

At his peak in the Seventies, Khashoggi was collecting commissions amounting to $100 million a year on Saudi defence contracts, mainly for Lockheed and Northrop. Born in Mecca and son of the king's physician, he cultivated a close relationship with Prince Sultan, the Defence Minister. When the boom collapsed, his investments in oil and property, mainly in Salt Lake City and the Sudan, also went sour: his personal fortune dropped in a decade from over $1 billion to a declared net worth of $54 million.

I asked him how had he coped with jail after riding so high on the magic carpet. "It's like being on a highway in the desert when your car suddenly breaks down. First you push, then you leave the car behind and walk across the desert for two or three days before you get back to civilisation. You're better off for the experience because you realise you have the will and the drive to endure hardships and overcome these setbacks.

"Prison was like that. After I got over the initial shock, my curiosity took over and I felt like a novelist taking everything in. I make friends easily, even in jail, and people would come up to me and tell me their stories. Some of these convicts had spent 20 years in jail and were facing new trials and maybe another 20 years, yet they were still fighting to get out of that awful place, if only to die in the street. Their will to fight was inspiring.

"I was arrested during Ramadan, on the way back to Mecca. It was time to talk to God, to pray, to read, to think about life. I believe God made this box, the body, and put some energy beams into it which we call the soul. We fast to purify our bodies so that the soul can communicate with its Creator. So the time I spent in jail was actually pleasant. It allowed me to do things which, because of my active life, I wouldn't normally do."

What was his worst disappointment? "It was a project to build a golf course, hotel, villas and apartment houses next to the Pyramids.

We had already signed the agreement for $1.5 billion and started building access roads, when President Sadat called me to say that a woman member of Parliament had had a dream in which the Pharaohs appeared to her and said foreigners (meaning me) were disturbing them. Believe it or not, the Parliament had a special session and voted against my project. President Sadat said he had to cancel it because he didn't want to cause any trouble for the Pharaohs. I lost 75 million bucks."

A.K. himself, it should be added, retains his own spiritual guru, the peripatetic Shri Chandra Swamiji, who was away when I called, consoling the recently defeated President Ortega in Nicaragua. I learned that his associate, the Mamaji, is in hospital after being arrested in New Delhi.

I asked Khashoggi about his public humiliations in the US. "It's like a movie to me", he said. "I knew this when I arrived here in handcuffs and they made me go to another car because the TV had missed the picture. Movies have a beginning and they have an end. Meanwhile, I play the part they have given me."

Going to court by subway rather than limo belongs, one suspects, to this public relations script. It is also, he insists, a more efficient way of getting downtown in the rush-hour. But the impression it gives of a man on his uppers — "Mister Moneybags Goes Down the Tube", as one newspaper put it — is some way off the mark, as any visitor to Olympic Tower can testify.

The Khashoggis occupy floors 46 and 47 in a 30,000 square foot duplex built for Aristotle Onassis. Clouds drift past the windows on a murky day. It is a palace in glazed walnut fit for Kubla Khan, lush with vegetation, including orchids and roses with no thorns, littered with silver, gold and marble knick-knacks, with ivory tusks, dragons, statues and bronzes, tables inlaid with lapus lazuli. Then there are the pictures in the inter-connecting sitting rooms: I spotted a Miro, a Pissarro, a Léger, two Monets, a Degas, two Gauguins — and that's not including the bedrooms.

In this context — the prisoner of Manhattan in his gilded cage — the famous swimming pool took on a homely look, surrounded by kiddies' red arm-bands, a jar of Johnson's Baby Lotion and two inflatable sharks. In court and out of it, the man himself exudes a cheerful relish and resilience that highlight the tearful gloom of the widow Marcos. On Monday evening, before the first day of the trial proper, he entertained family and friends at a chic Manhattan restaurant, tirelessly dispensing hospitality into the early hours, drawing out his guests on global issues, then leading a round of funny stories, as if he had no cares in the world.

Someone asked him how he felt about other people acquiring his abandoned luxuries — his legendary yacht *Nabila* (now owned by Donald Trump), his homes and private jets (and also, presumably, though the guest was too polite to mention them, what he used to call his "pleasure wives"). "I feel like Renoir must have felt. I am pleased that my collection is now giving happiness to others. Don't forget, I am a realist. Basically, I am not a materialistic person at all. The planes and the yachts were just business tools. I needed them then. I don't need them now."

By the second day in court, he was already feeling at home, beaming at his friends, shaking hands and pumping shoulders, telling jokes in the recess to a group of giggling schoolgirls. It was as if he was playing host at one of his fabulous parties. The court was a family outing for both defendants. A.K. was supported by his wife and son Hussein (studying finance at the American University in Washington), brother Essam (who trades in cement in Santa Barbara), sister Soheir and her daughter. Imelda had her son, Ferdinand Jnr, otherwise known as "Bong-Bong", her sister Portuna, daughter Irene and a craggy-faced nun called Sister Belarmine, who was said to be her half-sister.

Rival supporters of Marcos and Cory Aquino swapped slogans and insults outside the court. Inside, they sat in separate groups, rolling their eyes as evidence came out of the $220m Imelda is said to have salted away, two-thirds of it in America. "She used the Philippine National Bank as her personal piggy-bank," according to the prosecution, receiving fistfuls of dollars at her suite in New York's Waldorf-Astoria Hotel and spending it, not always shrewdly, on art and jewellery.

The main charge is that she and Marcos secretly brought into the States money fraudulently acquired in the Philippines and set up a "colossal cobweb of fraud" around the purchase of four prime Manhattan properties: the Crown Building on Fifth Avenue (opposite Trump Tower), the Herald Centre, 40 Wall Street and 200 Madison Avenue. Two banks are said to have been defrauded on loans.

Khashoggi, in a relatively minor role, is accused of "mail fraud" and "obstructing US justice" by assisting in the concealment of some of these deals and backdating a document. An earlier charge of racketeering has been dropped. Even so, he could face 10 years in jail. Asked bluntly by the *New York Daily News*, "Are you a crook? he said: "No — this is all an accident of life, like you fall and break your leg."

His leg, in fact, is a great focus of interest, since he carries an electronic tag round his ankle to stop him jumping bail. Imelda also attracts ankle-height attention in courts as everyone peers down at her feet (she was wearing only one pair of dainty black shoes when I looked).

Her counsel, the flamboyant Gerry Spence, is at pains to eliminate from the jury's mind the profligate image suggested by the shoe mountain discarded at the Malacanang Palace in Manila. She liked shoes, he explained, because she had gone barefoot as a child. Besides, most of them were gifts from the people and didn't fit her anyway.

Likewise, Khashoggi's lawyer, James Linn, is at pains to lift the prejudicial "arms trader" image from his client's shoulders, on the grounds that he acted merely as a broker on legitimate inter-government contracts that brought jobs to the US aerospace industry. The judge wearily interrupted that line of argument.

But Judge Keenan — a bald, peppery little man who seems fast asleep one minute, then scuttles along the bench in an erratically mobile chair that dwarfs him — holds most of his fire for Spence. The Westerner may have checked in his Stetson outside the courtroom, but not the matching style, and he provokes at least six bad-tempered rulings against him.

The infant Imelda, the unabashed lawyer reveals, once sang "God Bless America" to Irving Berlin, who was so moved by the experience that he sat down there and then and wrote a patriotic tune for Filipinos. His client sang, he added gravely, because she was hungry — to which my neighbour muttered: "She's eating well enough now, that's for sure."

One can only guess what the jury (six male, six female, six white; most of them blue-collar jobs) can make of all this. Or what they will make of the 300,000 documents filed in the case, including an "agreement of mandate" and a "declaration of trust" that seemed to have counsel confused. It took a week to empanel them as more than 30 were challenged. Both sides were seeking a jury that had never heard of Marcos or Khashoggi — surely an odd bunch of people in New York.

The US Government's case was put by a crisp modern-looking woman in a blue-check suit called Deborah Livingstone, who outlined a byzantine tale of "greed, theft, fraud and deceit" with not a hint of emotion. She didn't look as if she would be heavy on jewels or shoes herself.

The contrast with the hokey Spence was dramatic — and, I thought, revealing. Here were two kinds of America in conflict. Ms Livingstone belonged to a new, environmentally pure, post-Vietnam America that wanted nothing to do with these old corrupt dictators. It was as though a chapter of US history, a whole generation of foreign policy, was being fastidiously erased and put behind bars.

Spence, meanwhile, was dredging it all back up. The CIA must have known about Marcos buying into America, he claimed. It was creating a fund to fight Communism should he ever be overthrown. George Bush, first as head of the CIA and later as Vice-President, must have known and approved of the plan or it couldn't have happened.

Besides, he went on in his cowboy drawl, the Marcos fortune — what the US attorney called "bribes and kickbacks" — was "a way of life" in the Philippines. Paying Marcos was like paying their taxes. "People there see right and wrong in a different way than we see it".

The judge, who had been looking increasingly restless, pounced when Reagan's name came up. He asked, to general amusement: "Which count of the indictment does this involve?" There had been pre-trial speculation that Mrs Marcos might call the former President as a witness, to show that the ousted dictator had been given official refuge in America in 1986 at a time when his investments there were well known to the authorities and had even been written about in the press.

And there, I suspect, despite the judge's admonition, lies the whole crux of the case. How can politics be excluded from the trial of the wife of Ferdinand Marcos, when his whole career hinged on his country's relationship with the United States, in war and peace, over half a century? "Marcos may be dead, but he is on trial here," Khashoggi told me "They want to eliminate the Marcos money as a force in Philippine politics. That's what it's all about."

Khashoggi himself, whether the court likes it or not, raises another whole range of policy issues. This is the man who funded the first Irangate arms purchases for a branch of the American Administration — and claims he is still $15 million down on the deal. He knows where the bones are buried. "I always considered politics a waste of time and energy, but I have dealt with many politicians and heads of state. Of these, I'd say Nixon was a great man, one of the greatest Presidents America ever had."

I asked why he hadn't submitted to plea-bargaining with the US authorities, as others have advised him, or even done a midnight flit. His first answer – that his conscience and his pride would not allow it — carried more conviction when added to the second: that the case against him was so weak he felt sure he'd get off.

To judge from the opening statements, even a layman could see that the prosecution would be hard-pressed to prove that Khashoggi was dealing illegally with the Marcos family over the properties when he had other legitimate business arrangements with them, mainly over oil, which dated back to the early 1970s.

It may be hard to show that he defrauded anyone when he lost money on the deal. Or that a man in his exalted position, surrounded by accountants, would have had direct personal knowledge of documents. In the case of Imelda, the problem is to prove, now Marcos is dead, that she knew all that was going on. "Mrs Macros was a wife who did not know most of what he husband did, or the intricacies of finance," her counsel claimed. "Discuss," as they used to say in school exams.

Or try this one: when Marcos declared martial law, did that mean he was above the law himself, legally? And did he really lure a wily old bird like Khashoggi with the prospect of a ship of gold? And watch out for an exotic bit-player called Gliceria Tantoco, a mysterious lady who may have been acting for Imelda, but maybe for herself. The difference may make all the difference.

This case has everything a pulp fiction bestseller could possibly want: a celebrity cast, colourful settings, a tale of greed, power and corruption in high places. In addition, it raises some of the moral and political dilemmas of the second half of the twentieth century. It should run and run. All it needs is a happy ending.

The *Observer*, 1990

TEN MILES HIGH WITH IMELDA

Only once on the journey did Imelda Marcos flinch and lose her regal cool. It was when Adnan Khashoggi, the Saudi ex-billionaire, leaned across the aisle of his private DC9, tapped her right arm, the one bearing the knife scars from a failed assassination bid, and warned: "There are four US air force planes shadowing us all the way." He laughed as he said it, but she knew he wasn't joking.

Her four bodyguards stiffened and twitched the cabin blinds, No planes in sight. "You can feel the oppressive atmosphere," she shivered, "being watched so closely all the time." Khashoggi said that when he logged the flight and named his precious cargo, the official reaction had been "tense", as if they thought he might whisk her out of the country on his magic carpet.

During the rest of the flight — from New York to Providence, Rhode Island, to attend a celebration party by Doris Duke, the tobacco heiress, who had put up $5 million bail for Imelda — she talked non-stop at over 50,000 feet, recalling her past life with Ferdinand Marcos, the late Philippines President who died in exile in Hawaii in 1989, three years after being ousted.

She still talks about the reviled dictator with the pride of a woman in love — "he was a war hero, a scholar, a friend of the poor and he died of a broken heart." She carries around a printed card containing the last words he allegedly whispered while holding her hand on his deathbed: "Fear not, the truth will set us free."

Imelda and Khashoggi were both set free by a New York court, which acquitted them of racketeering and fraud charges over $222 million smuggled out of Manila and spent on art, jewellery and four Manhattan skyscrapers. Had the verdict gone the other way, she faced jail for 50 years and a $1 million fine. Hence the celebrations.

Before dancing with Khashoggi at a lavish party at a New York nightclub however, she had gone to St Patrick's Cathedral and crawled down the aisle on her knees to give thanksgiving. AK, too, had waxed religious, saying he would go to Mecca, where he was born, to thank God and the Saudi royal family for supporting him.

In keeping with the prevailing air of sanctity, Khashoggi brought along his guru, Sri Chandra Swamiji, spiritual adviser to the Sultan of Brunei, ex-President Ortega of Nicaragua and other rich clients. The bearded Swami, swathed in white robes, modestly admitted that he had correctly predicted three months before that Imelda would be acquitted on her sixty-first birthday.

The jury, drawn from a rare breed of New Yorkers who had never previously heard of the defendants — even though one of them was known as the world's richest man and the other as the world's greatest shopper — poured over complex legal documents for three months and then agreed with the judge, who had asked during the trial: "What is an American court for? What am I doing here at 40 Foley Square in New York trying a case involving the theft of money from Philippine banks?"

A juryman said of the trial afterwards: "It was the wrong side of the ocean." The female foreman added (American juries not having to swear a Trappist oath, as in Britain): "We didn't feel we could convict the woman just because she happened to be married to a person who might have been guilty."

Imelda said three of the jury went to see her on July 4th as an Independence Day gesture on behalf of all Americans for humiliating "an ally". One of the jury, a black woman, told her: "Every time they hurt you, they hurt me. You couldn't see, but I was crying for you."

Imelda says it was the attacks on her husband that caused her most pain and made her physically ill, once coughing up blood in the court. "Even Jesus Christ wasn't crucified again after his death."

With the strains of the trial over, the "steel butterfly" cut a very different figure from the weepy widow in court. She was controlled, assertive, more the strong woman who effectively ruled the Philippines in her sick husband's later years. An accomplished public performer from her early days singing to GIs, she offers a variety of faces to the world. The one I saw was softer, less puffy and coarse than often depicted, with the glow of the ex-beauty queen not far below the surface.

An aide hinted that the old prowling energy — two or three hours of sleep a night tiring out her staff — was beginning to seep back into her veins. How she wants to direct it remains unclear.

She said she feels grateful for the "purity of American justice" which allowed "the people, not the politicians", to decide her fate. But she clearly feels "betrayed" by the American government, which had welcomed Marcos and herself (in letters from Reagan and George Shultz) as "special guests", then given every assistance to Cory Aquino's attempts to recover through the courts up to $10 billion from Swiss banks and American investments.

"I was kidnapped by America", she says. "We were told we were being taken to my husband's home region, Iloco Norte, but instead we were flown to the US and made to suffer personal humiliations." This argument will soon be repeated in court as her lawyers try to clarify her status. One of them told me: "How can America claim to be supporting democracy in the Philippines when it is holding one of its most powerful political figures here against her will?" When I cocked an eyebrow at this — "She claims she's not a politician, just a widow" — he cocked one right back.

Did she help to finance the military faction that came within a hair's breadth of toppling Aquino, when 113 people were killed and about 500 wounded in street battles with tanks, mortars and rockets? She turned and looked me in the eye "I was too busying taking care of my dying husband."

Who arranged the killing of Benigno Aquino at Manila airport in 1983? The same direct look: "Cory Aquino knows the names. She has the files now. She also knows I had tried to help him before."

The Marcos trial took place in America because Aquino fears a "war of widows" and dare not allow Imelda into the Philippines, even to bury her husband (her ostensible reason for going back), because her presence might be a focus for dissident Marcos supporters, hundreds of whom paraded round Manila. The US government also wants to keep Imelda out as "a de-stabilising factor" just a year ahead of negotiations over renewing the lease on their military bases.

Whether Imelda's acquittal on criminal charges will now deter the Americans from pursuing the many actions due in the civil courts remains to be seen. "They have got a bloody nose," she says. "They should learn a lesson from this." Khashoggi adds: "They had a chance to produce their golden bullets at this trial and they didn't have any."

Imelda claims that Marcos was already a wealthy man when she met him, before he came to power, and that money he sent to America was his own, not rifled from the Treasury. From her handbag she produced dog-eared records of the Philippines central bank, purporting to show that Marcos had paid money into the national coffers.

I asked where the money came from. Gold trading mostly, she said, some of it from the legendary Yamashita treasure left all over the Philippine islands after the war by the departing Japanese. The court had heard tales of a "ship of gold" that Marcos claimed to have chartered. Khashoggi, for one, believes in the ship of gold.

What about the paintings and jewels? "Many of the paintings I bought were for our poor museums at home. As for jewels, I was blessed with a husband who was very generous to me." Then she pointed at me: "You British and Americans have never been invaded, so you don't understand that bank accounts can become just paper. Jewels are cash in my hand.

"I was brought up in wartime. My mother had a necklace that became our only wealth. Because my father was very tall — he was half Spanish — he always stood out in the Philippines, so they gave the necklace to me for safe keeping to wrap round my waist. It was made of small diamonds and we sold them off one at a time every few months to provide money to live.

"When the war ended, there was one diamond left. I asked my father if I could wear it, because people said I had a pretty neck. He then gave me a piece of advice I never forgot: "Never cry for that which cannot kiss or hug you back." He meant never be attached to possessions."

I felt obliged to point out that her image as "one of the world's great shoppers" (a phrase used by her flamboyant counsel in court) seemed to be at odds with this advice. Inevitably, the conversation got round to shoes. She pushed out her ankles to show me the neat black pair with brass buckles she was wearing.

"Shoes are not even my weakness," she claimed. "But as First Lady of a country you have a duty to promote its industries. One of our industries was leather. We got Australian hide and made it into shoes. There are 1,000 shoe factories in Marikina. They liked me to open them. Then they sent me their shoes as a present. Many did not even fit me. Many boxes were never opened. I had no idea there were so many in the Malacang Palace."

What did she now want from life? "I am an orphan from my country and a widow of my husband, I have not seen my daughter Emee for four-and-a-half years. I have not seen my grandchild. I don't miss things — I miss love and my loved ones. I want to bury my husband on his native soil and honour his memory."

Would she enter Philippine politics to honour his memory, maybe as a Presidential candidate in 1992? "When democracy is restored to my country, then I will go back. I want to dedicate my life to the poor people who loved my husband. A country needs a President, but it also needs a mother. That is where I could come in.

"I really wouldn't like to be in public life. It is terrible to feel like public property. I had a breakdown in my early years because I couldn't get used to losing my privacy. I would prefer the private sector.

"What you don't understand in the West is that the way we do things in the East is different. Not necessarily better or worse, but different. Right now the time is five o'clock in New York, noon in London and 6am in Manila. It is not better to be one time rather than another; they're just different.

"In my country we do not believe that men are weaklings who succumbed to Eve — the word itself being short for Evil. We believe men and women are equal but different. One is malakas (strong), the other magada (beautiful). Strength and beauty are in body, mind and spirit. Ferdinand and I were committed to that concept. God is made real for me in beauty. To reach for money and power is to reach for beauty."

Was she still reaching for power? She laughed: "Mr Donald, what I want is love, not power."

The *Observer*, 1990

NIXON COMES TO TOWN

Like a bad penny, former President Nixon turned up in town last week, fitting London between France and Spain on a promotion tour for his new book on World War Three.

His publisher, Lord Longford, anti-pornographer-royal and friend of the criminal classes, gave a dinner to honour the visit ("The Honorable

Richard Nixon", said the invitation) in the ballroom of the Hyde Park Hotel. Sir Charles Forte, the catering king, who owns both the hotel and the publishing firm, sat beaming on his left.

The assorted diplomats, tycoons, editors and other represen- tatives of the *demi-beau-monde* were fed on the best that Trust House Forte could offer: Mousseline de Truite Saumonee Pol Roger and Noisettes d'Agneau Jussière, washed down with Graacher Domprobst Beerenauslese 1976 and Chateau Montrose 1966. I sat between Margaret, Duchess of Argyll, and Colonel Jack Brennan, Nixon's self-styled Chief of Staff. She was a vision in red gauze, diamonds and pearls, with a gold handbag and a sprained wrist. The Colonel wore black; no diamonds, no handbag.

The Duchess professed herself an unashamed admirer of the former President. "I love the man, I love him," she enthused. She told him so before dinner. "Do you remember a crazy Englishwoman sending you cable after cable of support?" The former President thought hard. "No." he said finally, with characteristic wit, style and grace (and unwonted honesty).

The Duchess kept turning to me throughout Nixon's set speech with ecstatic stages whispers, like antiphonal responses. "Ours is not just a Western alliance, but a global alliance," said Nixon. "He's awfully good, isn't he?" whispered the Duchess. "We need to unite against terrorism — joint force, joint response," said Nixon. "Don't you love him, don't you love him?" trilled the Duchess.

Nixon's hazy rhetoric rolled on. "The Russians don't want war"... [long pause]..."but they want the world." The Duchess was now beside herself. "Kiss, kiss!" she cried. Nixon looked up in alarm. (Afterwards someone offered an explanation for this enigmatic cry. "She was trying to say Kiss-Kiss-Kissinger", he suggested — perhaps to acknowledge the intellectual source of Nixon's remarks.)

Hers were not the only noble tributes. Lord Longford referred to "President Nixon's wonderful book." ("I'm glad they're calling him President," the Duchess said.) Longford went on (rather ambiguously, I thought): "A child could understand the message of this book, but it would take a person of considerable intelligence to interpret the message." Nixon, he revealed, "is an established favourite with the British public."

Lord "Alf" Robens, former head of the Coal Board and much else — once proposed as a leading candidate for the Boardroom of Great Britain Limited — waxed lyrical. "After a long day," he declared, Mr Nixon appeared before us "with a freshness as though it was bright morning." And indeed the famous ski-jump nose, the Herblock jowls and the five o'clock shadow were strangely muted, as though his features had been drained of definition by the loss of power. The teeth looked different.

Lord Alf was "lost in admiration," he said, at Nixon's "outstanding career." He had achieved "more than any statesman anywhere in the world." By this he evidently meant things like ending the Vietnam war and opening the door to China — rather than, say, other aspects of his presidency.

Part of Nixon's appeal to the audiences, who still turn out for him — people who, given the choice, would probably prefer a strong bad man to a weak good man in power — is the contrast with the hapless Jimmy Carter. When the loyal toast was extended to "The President of the United States," a bluff businessman added loudly: "God help him!"

As if in reproof, the telephone rang outside. It was the White House on the line. Colonel Brennan took the message: "It's Brzezinski. Shall I talk to him or will you?" The ex-President pondered this grave decision. A finger shot out firmly: "You talk to him. But I'm available."

Eventually Nixon went out himself, followed by his bodyguard in a blue buttoned-down shirt, a Special Branch man with a fat cigar, Colonel Brennan — and a buzz of excited speculation. Something momentous was clearly going on.

When they returned, Nixon took the microphone. "You may be wondering why I went outside." Irreverent titters in the audience. "Not for the usual reason. It was Mr Brzezinski from the White House to tell me personally that a new Secretary of State has been appointed – Senator Ed Muskie of Maine."

Already Nixon looked a different man, more alert, less crumpled. Plugged in again to the power supply, he began visibly to shine. The old adrenalin was on the move.

Next to me, Colonel Brennan began to unwind. For a moment he had thought it was the President himself on the line, since Nixon kept saying "Sir". He had worked for Nixon for 12 years and had no complaints. "He's been good to me. I don't argue with people who disagree."

I confessed that my wife was among those who disagree. She disapproved of my going to the dinner. He sympathised sadly: "It's always the women. Whenever we get the old guys together for a Watergate reunion, it's the wives who try to stop them. Kalmbach made us pretend we'd bumped into him accidentally."

Did they still meet, then? "When we can. We saw Bob Alderman recently — he's doing well in business now. No, not Ehrlichman — he's dropped right out. Did you know Chuck Colson was in London this week to promote a sermon? I hear he's gone to Ireland."

An air of unreality was taking over, like a buzz in the ears. Emma Soames was ushered into the presence: *Alice in Wonderland* meets the Mad Hatter. Nixon suggested that her father might mediate with the Ayatollah (an intriguing prospect), presumably on the grounds that handling one Third World nut is much like handling another and that Iran is a place much like Zimbabwe (or "Boogieland", as Ms Soames described it in the *Tatler*).

Nixon fielded questions from the audience, mostly slow lobs that gave him a chance to demonstrate his genuine grasp of foreign affairs. Then a bearded man from the *Sunday Express* tried to bowl a faster one. Lord Longford's voice cut in loudly: "I don't know who this chap is, do you?"

Finally, Lord Robens rose to give fulsome thanks. "It's almost," he said wistfully, "as if you were a candidate." Suddenly, the creeping sense of unreality was overpowering. Time to go home.

The *Observer*. 1980

RUSSELL TOLD THEM ALL

In 1967, about six months after joining the Observer, *I was given exclusive access to a huge cache of letters by Bertrand Russell, which were being sorted for publication.*

Bertrand Russell questioned the existence of God at the age of 16 in a ruled black exercise book which he wrote in Greek for fear his Victorian family might ever find it. This exercise book, with a later translation in Russell's own hand above the Greek, has come to light among his voluminous letters and papers which are now being catalogued in London. It will be a prize item for collectors.

The papers — there are about 100,000 letters, nearly all of them unpublished, plus hundreds of manuscripts, tapes, journals, diaries, notebooks, honours and awards — have been sorted, filed and classified in a mammoth operation by Russell's literary agents, Continuum 1, in their offices near Oxford Street.

The documents, which include important additions to the Amberley Papers, the saga of the related Russell and Stanley families, will be sold in May — almost certainly for the kind of sum that only American academies are likely to afford. They shed a multitude of sidelights on the literary, political and intellectual life of Britain over three parts of a century. They are also a reader's delight. Last week I was granted an exclusive sight of them.

The archives establish Russell's claim to be the twentieth century's most prolific correspondent: he has written one letter for every 30 hours of his life, mostly to leading figures, on the central issue of the day. His life has been so long – 94 years, and his output shows no sign of slowing – that the causes he has publicly espoused range from Dreyfus to Lee Harvey Oswald and his correspondents from Tennyson to Sartre and Graham Greene.

The man who was told by Gladstone after dinner — "This is very good port they have given me but why have they given it me in a claret glass?" — has also discussed Vietnam with Harold Wilson, who became Prime Minister 155 years after Gladstone was born. His correspondence offers glimpses of a British lifetime that for variety, importance and span can be compared only with Winston Churchill's.

There are many surprises. To P.G. Wodehouse, creator of Bertie Wooster, we find this: "In common with the rest of mankind, I derive great pleasure from reading your books. But I have other claims to consideration more weighty than this: my name is Bertie; I had an aunt called Agatha and an uncle called Algernon; I came within an ace of being called Galahad, and my great-grandfather put up a plaque in his garden to commemorate a victory over his head gardener."

A surprise, too, is the evident depth of Russell's friendship with Joseph Conrad. It is unmistakable behind the heavily formal style of their exchanges, and is not without comic relief: Conrad appeared to be obsessed with the idea that Charles I had not been executed. The two men found immediate rapport and Russell's eldest son was named after the Polish novelist.

But as in many of Russell's relations with creative writers – with D.H. Lawrence, E.M. Forster, T.S. Eliot and Ezra Pound, as well as Conrad — his ideological commitment was a bar to total friendship. Conrad wrote to him: "The only ray of hope you allow is the advent of international socialism, the sort of thing to which I cannot attach any definite meaning. I have never been able to find in any man's books or any man's talk anything convincing enough to stand up for a moment against my deep-seated sense of fatality governing this man-inhabited world."

Lawrence distrusted Russell's political evangelism: "You are simply full of repressed desires, which have become savage and anti-social. And they come out in this sheep's clothing of peace propaganda." But with Russell the man and Russell the philosopher he was able to come to terms: "We are one in allegiance, really, you and I."

Forster could not accept Russell's credo that men must be made decent now to build a decent society in the future. But he admired Russell and in the files there is a dog-eared note written from Alexandria at the time of Russell's arrest in 1918: "In the middle of a six-course dinner at the club last night I was told you were in prison. This is to send you my love. I suppose they will let you have it when you come out."

But Russell's politics did find an echo in his time, if not among the politicians. George Bernard Shaw responded, even if he was sometimes "frivolous, cruel and rather stupid"; there were the Webbs, Harold Laski, George Santayana, Siegfried Sassoon — "the only thing worthwhile is the honesty of one's actions." There is even a letter to Maxim Gorky. Russell went to Russia in 1920 and recorded this impression of Trotsky: "Very Napoleonic. Bright eyes, military bearing, lightning intelligence, magnetic personality. Exceedingly good-looking. Would be irresistible to women, and an agreeable lover while his passion lasted. Vanity even greater than a love of power; the vanity of an artist or an actor." At the theatre Trotsky leaned across Mrs Philip Snowden during a tender love scene and startled her: "*There* is the great international language."

Russell found Lenin a contrast to Trotsky: 'Nothing in his manner or bearing suggests the man who has power. He looks at his visitor very close and screws up one eye.'

From Emrys Hughes in a guardroom at Rhyl, facing his third court martial for pacifism in 1917, comes this *cri du coeur* in indelible pencil on a lined sheet of paper: "I feel a thrill to think how we've challenged it all, refused to fight for the foul old ideas, and tried to show the way to a better life."

In letters to Russell, people seemed to feel a need to define their conduct; they are full of ethical maxims and calls to right action or duty, as if Russell were keeper of their consciences, father confessor to his age. Lawrence scrawled on the edge of a Russell manuscript: "Morality is one's inviolable sense of truth."

A young American poet signed himself Thomas Stearns Eliot to thank Russell in 1915 for the loan of his flat and to describe in formal bank-manager's English how he was teaching scripture and taking games at an Eastbourne school. In time the signature became 'Tom' and the syntax lost its polish: "I don't want my affairs to be buggered if I should die."

Eliot's mother, Charlotte, in a heart-to-heart with Russell, assuring him that there were French but no Germans in their ancestry and even, it seemed, a Devonshire grandfather, adds this little footnote to history: "I am sure your influence in every way will confirm my son in his choice of Philosophy as a life work. I have absolute faith in his Philosophy, but not the *vers libres*."

It was religion that parted him from Eliot, who wrote in 1927: "Your pamphlet seems to me a piece of childish folly. Why don't you stick to mathematics?" By 1949 all was forgiven — especially, it seems, childish folly. Eliot, congratulating Russell on his Order of Merit, added: "The Master of Trinity recommends safety pins in the ribbons, but a neat tuck on each side is much better."

In a letter from H.G. Wells, the progressive, the visionary, there is a profound note of pessimism at the last. He wrote to Russell in May 1945, calling himself President of the Diabetic Society: "The vast return of chaos which is called the peace, the infinite meanness of great masses of my fellow creatures, the wickedness of organised religion, give me a longing for a sleep that will have no awakening."

Ezra Pound writes from Italy in slogans that are simply mad, and cries: "God Almighty, why didn't I try to kick a little manhood into you?" Malinowski, the anthropologist, jokes: "I left my only presentable brown hat in your anteroom. I wonder whether since then it has had the privilege of enclosing the only brains in England which I ungrudgingly regard as better than mine." Rabindranath Tagore, the Indian poet, quotes at length from the Upanishad. Augustus John writes in old age and illegibly.

One of the most unlikely episodes revealed in Russell's papers is a correspondence with Sir Oswald Mosley. It appears that Mosley wrote to Russell in 1961 in an attempt to persuade him that their views on political action could be reconciled. Russell was cool but courteous through a number of exchanges; Mosley gradually warmed to the thought of an ideological merger, making cautious reference to remote ancestral connection through the Mitfords.

Finally Russell, in a devastating *coup de grace* that is unlikely to be printed in full in Mosley's lifetime, brought the affair to an end. "The emotional universes we inhabit are so different, and in deepest ways opposed."

For all his rejection of the assumptions of Victorian morality, Russell seemed to have carried with him through life a Benthamite faith in progress and the ultimate triumph of rationality. The pattern of his letters suggests that he has been engaged in a never-ending search for generals to help him fight the good fight for humanity's sake. But he never enlisted priests.

He looked first among the philosophers — Bradley, Moore, Whitehead, Wittgenstein; then to the artists — Lawrence, Forster, Conrad, Eliot; the scientists — Einstein, Niels Bohr and Max Born; and finally made a frontal assault on the politicians themselves — in long screeds to Nehru, U Thant, Ho Chi Minh, Tito, Nkrumah, Nasser, Kaunda, who reply with respectful interest, and to Presidents Kennedy and Johnson and the Queen, who barely reply at all.

Wittgenstein reached out to Russell in despair, "What I feel is the curse of all those who have only half a talent.' In Russell's rooms at Neville's Court, Trinity College, Cambridge, the Austrian philosopher several times threatened suicide. Later he confided: "I believe I have solved our problems finaly" [sic].

There are 60 letters from Wittgenstein in Russell's archives, about half of them in German. They are priceless to historians of philosophy, showing the way the two men spurred each other's genius. Russell later wrote to G.E. Moore of Wittgenstein's theories: "Whether they are true, I do not know; I devoutly hope they are not, as they make mathematics and logic incredibly difficult."

But Russell, pioneer of the twentieth-century revolution in philosophy, was able in the same lifetime to engage in a long and moving correspondence with the great metaphysician, F. H. Bradley, whose best work was written in the 1880s. It was a collision of two worlds: metaphysical Zeppelins punctured by the new fire-power of mathematical logic. Not surprisingly, it was Bradley who felt the pain.

The letters arrived regularly from Merton College, Oxford, or from Bradley's house in Weston-super-Mare, showing Bradley in an unfamiliar light as a shrewd and humble man. He, too, was reaching out to Russell, for assurance that his life's work had not been wasted: "I have been tending more and more to take refuge in the unknowable."

The letters are as many-sided as Russell's own life, and as important. His dry wit and laser-like concentration come across in almost every letter; there are few frills. Yet the man at their centre remains curiously opaque, a catalyst of passion in others, the elusive centre of a turning world. Only in martyrdom does the naked passion show, nowhere more explicitly than in this 1918 letter from Brixton prison:

"I want to stand at the rim of the world and peer into the darkness beyond, and see a little more than others have seen, of the strange shapes of mystery that inhabit that unknown night... I want to bring back into the world of men a little bit of new wisdom in the world; Heraclitus, Spinoza and a saying here and there I want to add to it, even if only ever so little."

The *Observer,* 1967

SNOOKER AT THE CAVALRY CLUB

Even by the high standards of snobbery in London clubs, the Cavalry and Guards in Piccadilly is something special — which makes its decision to desecrate its stately billiard room with a plebeian, not to say vulgar pool table all the more remarkable.

Captain Wetherall of the 20th Hussars, who founded the Cavalry Club in 1890, must be spinning in his grave. His club was noted for its hippophilia, still represented by its many statues and pictures of horses, and for its consumption of champagne — reputed to be the highest of any club in London.

When, in 1976, the Cavalry absorbed the Guards Club, it seemed a natural marriage, the Guards having been founded in 1810 by a subaltern in the Coldstreams called Jack Talbot, of whom it was said that "if he were tapped for blood, pure claret would come out", and who died, an empty sherry bottle beside him, at the age of 27.

Despite a members' revolt that failed to halt the merger, the clubs seemed to have settled down well together, their patrician poise undisturbed even by an IRA bullet fired from a passing car. It is a mystery why it has suddenly succumbed to the sleazy charms of pool, a pastime forever associated in the public mind with gum-chewing Americans in jeans and grubby T-shirts, surely the very antithesis of clubland chic.

When I put this to the club secretary, he admitted: "I can't give a satisfactory answer. It was suggested by a group of younger members. It's faut de mieux for the time being, until we identify somewhere else big enough to accommodate the snooker table".

There was once a move to have the snooker room at the Garrick Club converted into bedrooms, but we soon put a stop to that. I asked snooker-playing members there what they thought of the Cavalry and Guards' decision. "Incredible", said one, "it'll be bar billiards next". Another remarked: "It just shows what kind of people you get in the Army these days".

Reporting the news, the Peterborough column in the *Daily Telegraph* commented: "Pool is less satisfying a game than billiards or snooker, but perhaps appeals to military minds". This reveals total ignorance of the origins of snooker and of its indissoluble links with the military and with London clubs. In banishing the game like this, the Cavalry and Guards has betrayed a proud tradition and should be thoroughly ashamed of itself.

"Snooker" was army slang, a term used at the Royal Military Academy at Woolwich to describe a raw recruit, the lowest of the low. Around 1875 a young officer arrived at Jubbulpore from Woolwich to join the 11th Devonshire Regiment. When he missed an easy pot in the mess, a subaltern called Neville Chamberlain cried out: "Why, you're a regular snooker!"

The word and the game caught on among the British Army in India as Chamberlain moved on to the 12th Lancers in Bangalore, the Central India Horse, the Afghan war, the Burma campaign, the Kashmir Army, the Madras Army (which summered at the Ooty club in Ootacamund, now a shrine to snooker) and as secretary to Lord Roberts in the Boer War. He ended as Sir Neville Chamberlain, Inspector-General of the Royal Irish Constabulary and died at Ascot in 1944 at the age of 88.

Chamberlain had an historic meeting at the Calcutta Club in 1885 with the Maharajah of Cooch Behar and John Roberts, the leading English professional of the day, at which the rules of snooker were codified. Roberts then brought the game home to Britain.

Before then, unregulated forms of snooker, using many coloured balls, had been played in London clubs. In the Garrick Club snooker room there is a poster dated 1869 describing the rules of "Savile and Garrick Snooker". It declares: "In the event of the yellow ball being involved in a foul stroke, it is the custom for the watchers to cry out the word 'Bollocks!'"

There is also a large painting on the wall by Henry O'Neil, A.R.A. showing the game in progress. O'Neil, a Garrick member, includes himself in the canvas along with Trollope. His picture shows dozens of eager young toffs on a gambling night out, all straining for a sight of the green baize.

I was reminded of all this jollity the other night as I played for the losing Garrick team against the RAC, holders of the Hine Cognac inter-club trophy. The RAC billiard room in Pall Mall, with its five immaculate tables and its magnificent collection of snooker cartoons and memorabilia, puts the Cavalry and Guards to shame. (Pall Mall itself, by the way, derives from *paille maille*, an early form of billiards favoured by the French nobility).

Socially, I suppose, the rot began for snooker when the Duke of Edinburgh took the table out of the billiard room at Buckingham Palace, where it had been lovingly preserved by King George VI.

I urge the Cavalry and Guards, if only out of respect for its founders and for the memory of its long-dead comrades in India, to revoke this eccentric and degrading decision to abandon snooker for pool. If the noble game isn't safe at the Cavalry and Guards, then I fear we may all be snookered.

The *Evening Standard*, 1993

5 | OTHER PLACES

CHINA WITHOUT PREJUDICE

This article followed a visit to China in 1975 by British newspaper owners, led by Lord Rothermere, chairman of the Daily Mail *group. David Astor sent me in his stead. This article and one by Peregrine Worsthorne in the* Sunday Telegraph *were praised by Bernard Levin in the* Times *for "that rare thing, clear-eyed portraits of the country and its people, unswayed by any kind of prejudice" It presents a picture of China as it was, shortly before it was converted it into an ultra-modern superstate.*

From the air, Marco Polo's description of Peking can still be recognised, after 700 years: "The streets are so straight and wide that you can see right along them from end to end and from one gate to the other. And up and down the city there are beautiful palaces...The whole city is arranged in squares just like a chessboard."

The north-south axis, the massive Ch'angan boulevard, remains: the avenues have been widened and are washed clean every night; but the huge buildings of eyeless concrete designed by the Russians in the 1950s, cast a blight, and the old romantic alleyways have gone. The effect is joyless and dry, lacking human scale: a windy city, where no birds sing.

The birds were eliminated in a campaign in the 1950s. People banged dustbin lids and other cymbals all day long. The birds were too scared to come down and perished of exhaustion. They also banned dogs and cats in the cities; and it was so. A campaign against flies required over 500 million people to kill 10 flies each every day, which adds up. They also claim to have made headway in a campaign against rats. (But they missed one: I saw it running down a corridor in the Tung Fang hotel in Canton.)

The Peking Hotel turns out to be much like a four-star hotel anywhere else, with 12 gold pillars in the foyer, a billiard room, and champagne on ice in the bar. In the lobby there's a huge sign in English: "We have friends all over the world." As if to prove it, the red carpet is littered with polyglot delegations from everywhere — Yemeni generals, Romanian telegraph workers, the Finnish Academy of Sciences, Greater San Francisco Chamber of Commerce — mostly just hanging around, waiting for transport.

China makes about 20,000 cars every year, none for private use. We travelled in convoy in a model called the "Shanghai". It was a bulbous thing, a bit like post-war Standard Vanguard from the front, based on a Russian or Polish design. They also have a sleek black, curtained limousine that would cost Rolls-Royce about £15,000 to produce. These are for special friends like North Vietnamese generals, Albanian badminton players, and Professor J. K. Galbraith.

There is even a taxi service in Peking, but you have to book it from the hotel, which means they always know where you're going. This isn't true if you go out on foot, as I did in the early morning to take pictures, but they leave you little time for this. I did slip away one evening to an impromptu party in the diplomatic compound, and was driven back at high speed after midnight in an Arab's Mercedes. I don't see how my hosts could have known where I was; nor, however, am I sure that they didn't.

There are a number of restaurants around Peking, including the succulent "Peking Duck". There is one section for foreigners and one for Chinese; you can go into the Chinese part if you insist, but they're puzzled as to why you should want to. Our guide told us with great good humour that the Russian Embassy, frustrated at not being able to find anything out, sent two of its spies into one of these restaurants disguised as Albanians to talk to the locals. They were soon rumbled.

Wherever we went, we were met with large crowds of Chinese lining the pavements and clapping. Being applauded in the street was an unusual experience. What does one do? We decided to clap back, which went down very well (a tip for the Royal Family?).

One might expect, with the absence of private cars, a blissful return to the pristine, pre-industrial silence, before the tyranny of the internal combustion engine. Not so; not in Peking anyway, where a frightful racket starts at dawn. Trucks, trolleybuses and official cars honk the swarming cyclists out of the way, ignore traffic lights, and hog the crown of the road (alarmingly) in both directions at once. To an outsider, this smacked of privilege honking the under-privileged out of its arrogant path. When I said this, I was politely told that the cyclists saw it simply as road safety, which may well be so.

Bicycles cost about £40 in China; for most people, that is between two and three months' wages. The bikes are stiff and heavy, with big wheels; no gears, no drop handlebars. A bike, a sewing machine (about £30), a radio (£15) are the most prized possessions. On a tea plantation in Suchow we found that the four-bike family had arrived. TV sets cost about £80, having come down in price recently, but are out of reach to all but a privileged few.

★★★

We were taken to see the People's Daily in Peking, which sells four million copies and (unlike British papers) employs women in the printing works. Unlike British papers, too, it has a soldier with fixed bayonet outside the door.

The journalists, who work one-third of each year in the office, one-third in the countryside, and one-third at a cadre school for political education, earn an average of 80 yuan a month (£18); printers get £13. The highest-paid journalist gets 250 yuan and the lowest about 50 (a differential of 5:1, which is much wider than the spread of salaries on the *Observer*, for example). For comparison, a university teacher would get about 350 yuan a month.

On the way in, and again on the way out, we file into a long room with armchairs down each side and tables in front of them. On the wall are Chinese painting of birds, trees, flowers and misty mountains. Women pour hot water onto tea from massive vacuum flasks while we talk. Face flannels are brought round to refresh us. It is a soothing ritual, repeated everywhere we go.

★★★

The same ritual in the office of the Foreign Minister, Chiao Kuan-Hua, but the tea, the armchairs and the décor are of a higher order — in a pillared hall, with a soft pink carpet patterned with flowers, rather like the Mikado Room in the Savoy Hotel.

The Minister is a tall, relaxed smiling figure in rimless glasses, his hair, different shades of grey, brushed straight back. He smokes a lot, making points firmly with his cigarette. One felt he didn't need the interpreter but used the time to think out his answers. His expression moves quickly from laughter to an intense, slightly petulant expression, but his words are calm.

When he talks about America's recent war in Vietnam, there is a note of quiet exasperation, rather than anger or recrimination: "If only the United States had listened to our advice 20 years ago..." One senses suddenly that Chinese pride is a factor in their international affairs, not to be trifled with, a profound sensitivity about their dignity as an independent power.

Europe matters desperately to them, which is puzzling to a European. China's new heroes are those who support a strong, united Europe, whatever their views on social justice inside their own countries: Edward Heath was lionised here. Former friends like Tony Benn, whose opposition to Europe the Chinese found inscrutable, are regarded as frivolous isolationists whose views on worker control do nothing to redeem them. The British revolution was not, one felt, a matter of high priority in Peking.

★★★

Chairman Mao's portrait still dominates every room and every city square; his statue, like a white giant, is on display at airports, railway stations, and in the grounds of most schools and colleges. There are variations: Mao serene, Mao smiling, Mao relaxed in an open-necked shirt, Mao smoking, Mao clapping, Mao shaking hands, Mao in a white smock on an ethereal mountain top. None appear to have been taken in the last 30 years.

Opposite Mao in the city squares and party committee rooms stands a pantheon of four, whose coloured portraits never change: (left to right) Marx, Engels, Lenin, Stalin. Marx twinkles in his beard like a cross between Burl Ives and Santa Claus: Engels has a startled look, as if surprised to be there at all; Lenin is neat, stern and businesslike; Stalin wears an avuncular smile that will surely not survive Mao's death.

Mao is 81 and frail; he sees very few people, and then not for long. Chou En-lai is 77, with a heart condition; his doctors tell him not to see visitors for more than 20 minutes at a time, but he does. Much may depend on which of them goes first.

The third most powerful man in China is Teng Hsaio-ping, who was dragged through the streets behind a cart at the time of the Cultural Revolution. Teng is the best-dressed man in China, with a tunic of superior cut. (The "worst-dressed" award goes to Chiang Ching, Mao's wife, a former Shanghai actress, who sports a dated and baggy old tunic and cap, like a Carlisle railway porter's outfit, circa 1911.)

"The East is Red" is the tune blared out relentlessly over loudspeakers in the streets and parks. But the East isn't red; it's a sort of dull blue-grey. Only the tiny children are allowed to dress in bright colours. Most people, men and women alike, wear a shapeless cotton uniform, though party officials, and some of our guides, wore tunics of better material. After a while, the uniformity becomes oppressive on the eye.

★★★

Sightseeing: the Forbidden City, the Great Wall of China, the Ming tombs, all in quick succession and with jet-lag — a sure recipe for culture shock. You enter the Forbidden City from the huge Tiananmen Square, one side of which is the Great Hall of the People, through the Gate of Heavenly Peace. It consists of an endless series of Imperial Palaces with yellow roofs curling up to the sky, linked by massive courtyards and miniature gardens; we were rushed from the Hall of Supreme Harmony to the Hall of Middle Harmony, to the Palace of Heavenly Purity, to the Palace of Earthly Tranquillity, to the Hall of Mental Cultivation, the Palace of Abstinence, and so on till closing time.

The Great Wall of China is an hour's drive north of Peking, past prosperous-looking fields of wheat, sorghum and vegetables. It turns out to be a number of walls (2,500 miles of them) that were joined up about 200 BC to ward off the Huns, and kept in repair as a main line of defence until 1644, by which time the Manchu dynasty controlled the land on both sides of it.

There's a car park at the foot, full of coaches, with soft drinks for sale, just like Cheddar Gorge.

You can see the Wall best once you've climbed on top of it and walked up to one of the towers on the battlements: it drapes itself over one hill, then loops back down on the left, and suddenly reappears on the right, striding away.

The Ming tombs are approached via the Sacred Way, a long avenue guarded by gigantic statues of lions, camels, elephants, horses, fierce-faced generals and superior-looking animals that might have been invented by Tolkien. The Ming Emperors regarded their tombs as a life's work — in the belief, presumably, that no one would lavish such care on their memory as themselves. Anyone involved in the building of the tombs was buried with the Emperor as a security measure, some slaves being buried alive.

As a result, the entrance has been found to only two of the 14 tombs, and only one, that of Wan Li, the last of the Mings to die in his bed, has been excavated. There are great pavilions above, with the interment chambers far below, approached through forbidding leaden doors. The paranoid magnificence of the whole concept reminded me of Rhodes's grave in the Matopos Hills outside Bulawayo. I thought I caught a glint of approval, even envy, in the eye of the leader of our delegation, Vere Harmsworth, a scion of the great Napoleonic Northcliffe.

Personally, I must admit to some disappointment at the bareness of the tombs. Most of the treasures have been taken away and replaced with Soviet-style political texts and paintings, pointing up the imperial monstrosity of the exercise, in case anyone happens to be impressed. Inside the main burial chamber a wall carries this reflection: "It took the wheat ration of 10 million Chinese to build this tomb."

We heard about some unmarried couples — evidently underawed by all this — who had been caught in the Ming Tombs making love. They were publicly disgraced in the local Press; one of the few clues to sexual habits in Mao's China, a subject of endless speculation. Is there pre-marital sex? Have the young really been persuaded to give it up, or put it off, until they reach the official age for wedlock — 27-28 for men, 25-26 for women? Can human nature be so changed?

How can one tell? Contraception and abortion are said to be freely available; but statistics are not. On the one hand we are told: sex is a crime, the first sign of revisionist tendencies — no sex, please, we're Chinese. Then old China-hands talk of Shanghai's "air of sensuality" (which I must say, eluded me totally), how senior officials are said to keep mistresses, how the pill is prescribed for unmarried girls.

The truth is probably that in the countryside people do marry younger, in the traditional way (partly because they outgrow their parents' houses); and in the towns much will depend on the attitude of the local revolutionary committee. In any event, Chinese don't need permission to get married. The age limits are simply guidelines which good party members are likely to observe more closely than others.

What hits a Western visitor between the eyes, especially if he came in via Hong Kong, is the absence of any kind of sexual display, no make-up, women in the same shapeless clothes as men, unisex haircuts, and not a leg in sight; no dirty bookstalls, no commercial exploitation of any kind; in film posters the women are shown as handsome, certainly, with glowing health and sparkling teeth, but in a heroic, uninviting posture, looking half-right and ever upwards, towards a new production target.

★★★

One of our guides had been to London for delivery of Mr Heath's pandas. He had been amazed and rather shocked at the fuss in the papers. Zoo politics is serious business here. We ask after Mr Nixon's musk-oxen, which he brought here as a gift. One of them was reported to have been getting progressively sicker during the Watergate crisis. Questions about its health are politely evaded. I think it must be dead.

★★★

Dinner with the British, who now keep a low profile in Peking, mindful of the humiliations suffered a few years ago when the embassy was burnt down, the charge d'affaires beaten to his knees and at least one embassy wife stripped naked by marauding Red Guards. The British contingent finally fled to the Finns, who commendably took them in.

★★★

"In agriculture, learn from Tachai", says one of Mao's more insistent Thoughts. We were there to do just that. Tachai is a production brigade in an agricultural commune in Shansi province, an overnight train ride from Peking. It is bleak beyond words. In winter the temperature drops to 22 degrees below. Our time there was like two days in the life of Ivan Denisovich — no heating, cold water shaving, slop buckets etc. We warmed ourselves with hot brandy and slept in People's Liberation Army greatcoats.

The story of Tachai is a hymn to the spirit of self-reliance and illustrates Mao's concept of life as a heroic revolutionary struggle — an idea that the peasants find easy to follow. The ground is of unyielding rock; year after year the crop was destroyed by a series of natural disasters; as recently as 1963 the houses were washed away by a mountain torrent. Today it is a model commune, with neat terracing, a reservoir, a hospital, tractors, and an impressive crop yield.

The transformation, as on an Israeli kibbutz, was brought about by toil and faith. It was led by a devoted Maoist, Chen Yung-kuei, a peasant who has been made Vice-Premier of China for his pains. He sits now on the rostrum at Peking receptions, a white Shansi cloth round his head, looking rather puzzled. We are shown a tree under which, according to party legend, landlords used to whip the peasants in the old days. Children are taken there for a lesson.

How much does a Tachai peasant earn, scratching at the rocky soil in the bitter dawn for six days a week? He gets his ration of wheat and rice and a cash payment of about 500 yuan a year (£120), which compares badly with tea plantation workers we meet later in an altogether softer billet in Suchow.

"To each according to his work" is the theme, not the more radical "To each according to his need" — that comes later, we are told, when the ideal Communist society has been achieved. Pay is calculated on a points system according to the number of days worked and the nature and effort of the tasks. The commune's income depends on how much it produces to sell to the State; the revenue, after deductions for costs, welfare and a capital accumulation fund, is divided out among the peasants according to work-points.

So wages depend, not on the State, but on the success or failure of the commune, which must lead to wide anomalies around the country. When I say this, I am primly told, "The purpose of work is not to earn wages", which puts me in my place.

★★★

Nanking is greener than Peking, a garden city, with 18 million trees (so they say) and a shiny new airport, all glass and wasted space. Two MiG fighters take off under us as we land.

It is an ancient city, going back 2,400 years and was Chiang Kai-shek's capital. We visit the elaborate tomb of Sun Yat-sen, leader of the movement that overthrew the Manchu Empire in 1911. We are amazed to learn that Sun Yat-sen's widow is still alive and living in Peking. She is one of the famous Soong sisters, who were educated in the United States. Her sister married Chiang Kai-shek (some say at gun-point). I'd like to read their memoirs.

We visit Nanking Observatory in the Purple Mountains outside the city, where the lecture goes something like this: "Before liberation we had only 10 people working here and very few telescopes. Thanks to Chairman Mao, we now have over 200 staff and many telescopes. Since the Cultural Revolution, when our political consciousness was raised and we realised the errors of Liu Shao-chi and Lin Piao, we have used self-reliance instead of foreign help. As a result, we have discovered two tiny planets which had never been recorded before."

"Self-reliance" is also the theme of the Nanking-Yangtse river bridge, a mile-long double-decker. The Chinese are very proud of it, and with reason. It was started in 1960 to Soviet specifications; then came the Sino-Soviet split and the Russians tore up the contract for supplying the special steel. "We were sabotaged by the Soviet revisionist clique," said the unsmiling girl who gave us the lecture. But SR saved the day again, forcing the Chinese to make their own steel. As Chairman Mao puts it, "Bad things can be turned into good things."

One reflects that Mao's heroic struggle has become a kind of national metaphor into which almost any human situation can be fitted. But at least they have a national metaphor, and it seems to work. And there's nothing wrong with self-reliance, after all. Nor, perhaps with self-criticism, another phrase we keep hearing. One of our group likens this to group therapy, which strikes me as a shade fanciful. In practice, one suspects, it means lying to curry favour once you've been caught stepping out of line. But at least it's apparently bloodless.

Nanking at night has a relaxed Mediterranean air, people lounging at street corners, cycling lazily home, or talking in small cafés — so different from Peking, where people move in a purposeful way, as if they know where they're going.

★★★

In the morning we drive out of the city into the hills, past peasants with cigarette holders, chickens scratching at the foot of banyan trees, and water buffalo stumbling stupidly round the muddy paddy fields. We reach a gentle fold in the hills, where a row of chairs is prepared for us. A hawk hovers in the stillness overhead.

We are there to see Nanking Rail Vehicle Plant Militia at target practice. Girls and boys aged between eight and ten, called Little Red Soldiers, fire tracer bullets from automatic rifles that are almost as big as themselves.

A Chinese-speaking member of our group examines the targets through binoculars. They show ugly masks on Soviet-style helmets, on which is written "Oppose the Soviet Union and Protect against Revisionism". All enemies dispatched, the children jump smartly to their feet, dress from the right, about-turn, march back to their places with clenched fists. Their faces are without expression. They are the same age as my children, who can barely clean their own shoes.

Every factory and commune in China has its own militia, who receive weapons training for part of a day each week, and for one week each year. They also do anti-aircraft exercises, learn to swim in full kit and have courses in political education. This covers men between 16 and 40 and women between 16 and 35, so the number of Chinese who are (theoretically) competent marksmen, if you include the Dad's Army of over-40s, amounts to more than 500 million.

We go under the streets of Nanking, into a concrete warren of tunnels that is described as an underground bomb, fall-out and bio-chemical warfare shelter. This one — with electricity, telephones, a store for water and grain, an engineering workshop and an air purifying plant — has room for 4,000 workers and 10,000 dependants; there are said to be others covering the whole town, some bigger than this. In the shelter I ask a man playing Chinese chess who he thinks is going to attack him. "The Soviet socialist imperialists," he replies without hesitation, surprised at the foolish question.

Back at the rail vehicle plant, the genial elderly chairman of the revolutionary committee hands over, after the opening pleasantries, to his lean young deputy, who has an impressive grasp of statistics. Since liberation, the workers had made large-scale innovations, he said, increasing productive capacity by 11 times, output by 13 times, floor space by 3-6 times, capital equipment by 4-5 times. Since the Cultural Revolution in 1968, there had been further improvements (including, one suspects, the emergence of men like him).

His earnest speech was enlivened by the ill-timed whistles of old steam trains outside, echoes of another age, like the Chattanooga choo-choo, and by the sound of workers, including girls, clearing their throats without inhibition into spittoons. (The Chinese smoke too much).

Then, suddenly, a phrase in his speech stood up for inspection. Political education was needed in the factory, he said, to rid the workers of "bourgeois ideology". What form did this bourgeois ideology take? we asked. There were children of former landlords and rich peasants, rightist elements, who were trying to influence the thinking of the young, he said fiercely. This glimpse of class struggle in the factory was all we got; he probably thought he'd said too much already. The party heavies around him seemed to think so too.

★★★

In the English class at Nanking teacher training college, there was a coloured picture on the blackboard of an idealised family group. The students were asked to stand up and identify them — which they did with phrases like "He is a worker", "She is a Little Red Soldier". Then a pretty girl with pigtails went out to the front and pretended it was her own family: "This is my father. He is a worker. This is my mother. She is a teacher in a middle school. Both my parents worked for the revolution, studying the works of Marx and Chairman Mao."

The pride-in-family-background theme, a sort of Chinese Janet and John, was developed as other students came forward, "My family lives a happy life too. My father is a carpenter and is party secretary for the brigade. He works hard for the party and the people. All the people in my family study and work hard. We all love Chairman Mao."

This sounded surprisingly like the beginnings of a new form of family snobbism, surely at odds with egalitarianism. One longed for someone to come forward and say: "My mother's a tart and my father's a slob and a layabout, but I'm doing my best in the circumstances".

In the art class there were Soviet-style posters of men working cheerfully in the fields and women heaving picks mightily. But there were also paintings without progressive content, which seems to be allowed — of people if they're happy, of scenery if it's beautiful, and of flowers and birds if they're Chinese. Two old artists were doing classical calligraphy, which looks a bit like a Picasso drawing.

An evening's entertainment in Nanking. The standard was set by a remarkable opening tableau in which children rode mini-bicycles on top of revolving umbrellas that were held up by hand. A juggler hurled vases around, catching them in the back of his neck, balancing the rim of huge plant pots on his temple; a magician made goldfish in bowls come and go, ending with dozens all over the stage.

Girls did amazing things on a bicycle perched precariously on a sort of ironing-board; then 14 people clambered aboard one bike while it raced around the stage; there were whistlers who mimicked birds, galloping horses and a car crash; and a resounding finale in which acrobats, dressed up as lions in pairs like pantomime horses, leapt and fought to the crashing of cymbals.

★★★

By slow train to Suchow, past flat fields and deserted pagodas. The train has hard seats like French third class. It's worse for the Chinese, who are segregated from us and lie around on benches reading papers and drinking tea. The trains are green, and have a viewing platform at the back, as in Westerns. Endless music and hectoring in Chinese on the loudspeaker in the compartment; I lack the courage to pull the plug out.

Suchow is small and pretty, with white-painted houses. There are rickshaws with paying passengers; a few white pith helmets; washing hangs on bamboo poles in the street; water runs between the houses; there are dozens of small shops selling meat, bread, clocks; carts go by, filled with live ducks or skinned pigs' heads, pulled by ropes round the necks of unliberated coolies; a woman sits on the pavement reading a newspaper to her husband.

Suchow is said to be famous for China's most beautiful women: they must have been hidden from us. The claim is more believable of their food, the best we have in China. There's a tomato soup that is set on fire; we eat crab, shrimp, rabbit, lake fish, pork, chicken and a pigeon's egg at one sitting (and suffer no ill effects).

We visit a tea commune outside the city. Women workers are strongly in evidence here, clipping jasmine for the tea, dredging a river, shovelling coal, one with a trowel on a building site. They also make carpets. We are taken for an outing in a concrete boat.

The ideological flavour is strong, like the tea. At the commune school, songs like Methodist hymn tunes drift out of the music class. One song, written after the fall of Saigon, is called: "Who in the world is afraid of American imperialism?"

Afterwards, we sit in a cool, landscaped park called the Garden of Humble Administrators. There are works by Mao and humbler poets on the walls of tea rooms in all public places. They look nice: one wonders why we don't do the same with poems of Betjeman or Mary Wilson.

★★★

"In Heaven they have Paradise, on Earth we have Hangchow." Our guide's lyricism is undeterred by the rain sweeping over the city. Very few visitors are allowed into Hangchow these days, and our own visit wasn't confirmed until the day before. Some say this is because Mao lives here; others say there's some sort of "trouble". I ask if the Chairman has a house in Hangchow: "Yes." Then a pause and a correction, in case I get the wrong idea: "The State has a house here, which Chairman Mao uses sometimes."

The lake, set in mountains and trees, is quite beautiful: the Chairman has good taste. We took a boat on it; the weather was so bad we wore macs and warmed our hands on cups of tea, as on a day trip on Lake Windermere; the ladies in the party squealed with bourgeois delight at desirable lakeside properties that needed only a lick of paint, a garage, and a boat moored at the front to look like Virginia Water.

After dinner three of us walked by the lake. The soldier at the hotel gate used his telephone as we left and again when we returned. Young couples parked their bikes by the lake and sat on benches looking across the water in the moonlight — they may have been holding hands, we couldn't see. It was romantic, magical, reassuring.

It was reassuring, too, the next morning, to get a glimpse of geraniums among the plants and mini-trees in Hangchow's answer to Kew Gardens. They have a great pride in their blooms and in the massive carp in their rock pools. But they are not much given to lawns. The only serious one left in China is at the British embassy in Peking — lawns, presumably, being suggestive of frivolous bourgeois values like deckchairs and idleness.

In the ornamental gardens of Hangchow our demure lady guide made her one stunning lapse from perfect demeanour. She turned to the wives in the party, pointed vaguely off-stage, and remarked: "Ladies, I think it is time for you to shit."

★★★

On the train into Shanghai we see a wall poster: "We want worker representatives, not family representatives" — a whiff of nepotism in Shanghai railway yard? I look up from my detective story and note that our lady guide is reading "*Communique of the Second Plenary Session of the Tenth Congress of the Committee of the Communist Party of China*", or some such thriller. A penance for her earlier lapse?

We are given lavish helpings of excellent Chinese beer. I ask the guide if British delegations drink the most: "No, the Australians."

I awake at six to a rusty old record of the Internationale, but Shanghai has woken up earlier. Men are hand-wrestling in the street in a light-hearted way, while others argue over bicycles. It is a sprawling, ramshackle city, with scruffy grey buildings and hundreds of small shops, a bit like Cairo or the poorer parts of Casablanca. I was reminded of the US Senator who said in 1940: "With God's help, we will lift Shanghai up and up, ever up, until it is just like Kansas City."

Our hotel used to belong to the Sassoon family. Service in the panelled dining-room has an air of the ancien regime: one feels one might be offered tiffin; we play billiards. Later, we pass the Peace Hotel, where Noel Coward wrote "Private Lives".

Sterner things are in wait for us. We visit a revolutionary street committee which runs a massive housing complex for 54,000 people in 670 blocks of buildings. They run their own schools: four middle schools, seven primaries, nine kindergartens. They have a hospital and seven clinics. They stress what they call three-in-one education — by teachers, parents and retired people. Women retire at 55 (50 if they're in manual work) and then help out in projects like this at 70 per cent of their previous salary. They have an intriguing phrase — "former housewives" —to describe the women who run the canteen, do the cleaning, and mend clothes, etc.

★★★

We visit the home of Chen Tsuei-ying, aged 47, who tells us about the housekeeping. She earns 60 yuan a month in a leather factory; her husband, Lu Yueh-kun, 51, earns 90 yuan a month in the same factory. A son earns 20 yuan a month as an apprentice in a steam turbine factory, where he lives during the week. She and her husband share two rooms with their two teenage daughters, who are at school. For this they pay about 12 yuan a month in rent, gas, water and electricity. They bank 50-60 yuan a month (Chinese banks pay 3.25 per cent interest.) They cycle to work six days a week. On their day off, her husband "smokes and drinks wine", while she listens to theoretical broadcasts and studies the lives of good people (so she said).

The tiny room we were in had a double-bed, wardrobe, two cabinets, two radios (one a transistor), a clock, a table and four chairs. It was cheered up by a world map, family snapshots, and a small bust of Chairman Mao. In the other room there was a double and a single bed and a bicycle in the corner. She shared a kitchen, washroom and bathroom (including a stone bath) with another family. There was strip lighting, no heating.

Medical treatment is free for workers, who pay into an insurance scheme. Parents pay half the medical costs of children. A child's appendix operation would cost the parent 5 yuan (just over £1). There are 56 days' paid maternity leave.

Mrs Chen said her father had been a farmer who couldn't support his family and came to Shanghai to work in the docks. They had lived in a straw hut on the edge of the city; the children slept under the bed. Her two elder sisters had been sold to a landlord 50 years ago and she hadn't seen them since. She concluded: "Thanks to Chairman Mao, we lead a happier life."

★★★

The Wen Hui Pao newspaper in Shanghai, which is printed in what looks like a former nightclub, sparked off the Cultural Revolution. But its idea of "culture", let alone "journalism", turned out to be very different from ours. This became clear at a dinner the newspaper gave in our honour. Peregrine Worsthorne, who had been growing visibly frustrated at his inability to engage our host in serious conversation, seized on a chance remark that the paper gave coverage to the arts. "That's very interesting," he said. "Our friend here from the *Observer* comes from a paper which also pays special attention to the arts.

"I wonder," he asked innocently, "if our friend here were to write down the names of five works that represent British culture, would you then write down the five books of Chinese literature that you think we should read?"

Casting around my mental lumber-room, I came up with Chaucer's *"Miller's Tale"*, *"As You Like It"*, *"Pride and Prejudice"*, Newman's *"Apologia"*, and *"Lucky Jim"*. As afterthoughts I offered *"Love's Labours Lost"*, Conrad's *"Nostromo"* and Auden's poem on the death of Freud. Our host read the list seriously and consulted his colleagues. After some hectic discussion in Chinese, they told us politely that they were unable to do as we asked, as they couldn't agree on five titles of sufficient ideological purity. (Mao's name didn't come up at all.)

★★★

We met our first Chinese trade unionist in a Shanghai shipyard. What did he do, I asked, if he didn't negotiate wage rates? Wages are fixed according to an 8-grade system, depending on the job. The rates were changed in 1960, 1966 and 1972. In this shipyard the wages ranged from the Chief Engineer's 210 yuan a month to 40, with an average of 70: again, as wide a spread as in the capitalist West.

He organised welfare and recreational facilities, he said, "and exposed any contradictions that might exist among the workers". What contradictions had he found in this shipyard? the Reuters man asked craftily. The answer was very long and fervently expressed, involving frequent reference to Chairman Mao. The trade unionist, who was very young, was supported throughout by a sweet-looking girl in pigtails who never stopped smiling. They were clearly a stronger moral force than the notional bosses.

For a start, they said, the workers had discovered that the design of a ship was "conservative and reactionary", in that it had two cables where only one was needed. So they protested to the Chief Engineer, who agreed, thus saving the State many yards of wasted cable. Then the workers noticed that there were four lights in each cabin where two would do, so this was changed too. They spotted also that there were electric fans in the cabins as well as air-conditioning, so the fans had to go. What if the air-conditioning broke down, we asked? Answer: "Before liberation it might have broken down, but not now." Silly question.

★★★

The pick of Shanghai's children — *la crème de la crème* — go to a Children's Palace after school and on Sunday mornings to develop their talents (no trouble about "selection" here). They sing or dance or paint or play musical instruments, table tennis, gymnastics or learn to assemble a TV set or a model aeroplane or a simple electronic calculator. They are all taught to do something as the main part of the curriculum, rather than absorb theoretical knowledge, which struck one as a major difference from our system.

In the ping-pong hall the tables stretched as far as the eye could see. They were like robots, all playing exactly the same shot, the forehand drive (no backhand at all), so that play went on endlessly from one diagonal to the other until someone hit the net. Vere Harmsworth patted lobs to a little girl who serenely disdained to destroy him.

★★★

At an industrial exhibition in Shanghai, an exquisite form of Chinese torture, we were introduced to hydraulic free-forging presses, laser scalpels for eye surgery, high precision lead screw lathes, and similar delights, but the Chinese haven't the same relish for all this as the Russians who built the exhibition hall.

There is a display of consumer goods being made for export — including skiing equipment, textiles (good stuff badly designed), mopeds, and grand pianos — but one feels they haven't really got their heart in all this either.

I asked about the mopeds: why didn't we see more of them all over China, as one does in Arab countries? Our guide replied: "If some people have mopeds, everyone will want mopeds. Then they'll want cars, and before we know where we are we'll have a capitalist system." He has a point.

★★★

It was a point that came back forcefully in Canton, home of the twice-yearly trade fair. Canton is a city of huge department stores, NAAFI-like hotels and imported Japanese cars, quite unlike the rest of China; the people look different too, in white shirts and blouses in the sticky heat.

Foreign businessmen come and go by train from Hong Kong talking about exchange rates and order books. As I went out, Lord Thomson, the newspaper owner, was on his way in. He is a "friend of China" and takes the waters with his daughters at a soda spring near Canton.

It is a fast train to the border on the Chinese side, past fields of rice, wheat and bananas. We debouch at the border station, cross a short track of rail that is overhung with a semi-circular aluminium roof, and find ourselves in Britain. Instead of Chairman Mao, there's a Union Jack and pictures of the Queen.

The train is much slower and dirtier on the British side, making frequent suburban stops, like the outer edges of the Northern Line. And so to Hong Kong, where civilisation is represented by Coca-Cola signs and traffic jams, lost luggage and bent policemen, money-grubbing porters and cross-looking girls in mini-skirts.

★★★

What, after three weeks, are we to make of it all? When we discussed it among ourselves, Worsthorne extolled freedom of the individual above all other values, comparing the regimentation of the Chinese unfavourably with the waywardness of Indians. But what, some of us replied, is the value of that freedom to the millions who die of starvation?

Is that the bleak choice, then: to starve in Indian chaos or eat in Chinese thraldom? Or should China be compared, not with India, but with Japan? Perhaps it should really be compared with a hypothetical abstraction: the China it might have been under a different regime since 1949.

China's achievements since then are undeniable. They have fed, housed, clothed and educated themselves with minimum help from outside. There is a State guarantee against starvation for a quarter of the world's population, and against homelessness and unemployment — guarantees that work. R.H. Tawney wrote of the Chinese peasant after a visit in 1930: "He is a man standing up to his neck in water, so that even a ripple is sufficient to drown him". Life is still hard for the Chinese peasant, but the State keeps his head above water.

The Chinese have done what free Africa has conspicuously failed to do: conquered ignorance, poverty, disease (before Mao, China was riddled with VD and drugs, which have both simply vanished). No wonder the Third World looks to China.

And yet, for half a century now, Mao has been so taken up with winning a civil war and then creating the political inspiration and method for the eating-feeding-clothing-housing side of things that any questioning of the system, any attempt at the free play of intelligence or imagination, has had to be suppressed. The result, it seemed to me, has been like keeping a nation of children in a giant schoolroom, from which the mysteries of adult life, the terrors of choice, have been rigorously excluded.

Plainly, once basic needs have been met, the human personality must be given free rein if the society is to be civilised — for reasons of humanity and probably, too, for reasons of efficiency. Can China allow this to happen without falling apart? The cultural revolution seems to have been partly about this; Mao's last attempt to stop the rot towards revisionism. After Mao's death, most China-watchers put their money on revisionism.

There are things we can learn from Mao's China: their sense of communal inter-dependence, which acts as a check on personal consumption, their humanising procedures within organisations, which relate an individual's effort to the life of the community and give him a sense of purpose. Some such revisionism could usefully go on here.

Finally, one was left wondering how long there is going to be such a sharp and compelling choice between capitalism and Communism, which will interact with each other increasingly. We seem to be entering a world in which the absolutes of both are rejected, where frozen political creeds are giving way to systems that are constantly tested by men's understanding, where collective purposes are pursued without the loss of liberty and common sense, and where, ultimately, certain private values should be placed above everything else. China has found an answer for itself, perhaps, but not for us.

The *Observer* Magazine, 1975

IT'S NOT SO EASY BEING A JEW

This article was written in 1980 after a ten-day visit to Israel, one of six I made to the country, meeting five different Prime Ministers. I reproduce it here because it records Israel as it was at the time and was praised by both Jewish and Arab readers.

A NEW Israeli joke. A member of the ruling party is haranguing his colleagues: "Things have come to a terrible state, my friends. The whole world is against us. The Arabs are getting stronger every day. Our economy is in ruins. Inflation is over 100 per cent. Strikes, demonstrations, everywhere. I tell you," he concludes, thumping the table, "none of this would be happening if Begin was alive!"

It is a curious fact that the Israeli Prime Minister, whose name has been denounced in every language on earth, seems almost invisible inside his own country. Nobody seems to know him well. I asked one of his closest associates, a leading man in the Herut Party who has worked with him for nearly 40 years, what Begin is really like. "His wife knows him," he said. "Nobody else."

Israeli Cabinet meetings must be the longest and leakiest in the world: Rabin, when he was Prime Minister, once tried to make his Cabinet take a lie-detector test. Every member has a right to speak, so they go on for about 10 hours. Begin's handling is said to be patient and self-effacing, with the iron will under control. But he can't shut his Ministers up, either during or afterwards.

Dissatisfaction with the Government is expressed loudly on all sides. On the day I arrived the Peace Now movement had a protest that linked arms all the way from Haifa to Jerusalem. Then 4,000 settlers, taking the opposite view, marched on the Knesset (Parliament) demanding formal annexation of the West Bank. Twenty started a hunger strike.

And that was just Israelis. Palestinians had their own marches and demos in Nablus, Hebron and Jerusalem. When I referred to all this on a journey through the West Bank, my military escort was subdued. Then he heard a radio bulletin in Hebrew — and his face lit up. "Not only riots in Nablus," he chuckled, "but in Britain too!"

Another Israeli joke. Two old friends meet in Tel Aviv. One is very depressed. "I'm thinking of leaving, Moshe, back to New York."

"But why, Elie?" his friend asks.

"For two reasons. This Government is hopeless. They can't solve our border problems, they can't keep prices down, they can't do anything."

His friend interrupts. "But Elie, all this will soon change. Begin's government can't last. Then we'll have Shimon Peres and the Labour Party back again."

"And that's my second reason for leaving."

Peres met me in the Labour HQ — as if to prove a point, since his hold on the Labour leadership is not secure. The main threat is from Rabin, his old enemy, who snatched the leadership from him in 1974. Peres and Rabin hate each other. In his memoirs Rabin sees the hand of Peres raised against him at every stage of his career, including his ignominious fall from office over his wife's illegal bank account. It's a bit like Thatcher and Heath.

Rabin is a slow, dignified man, with a rather weary air, given to careful exposition. He is said to be bad at nursing politicians and to see too many sides to every question. He smokes non-stop. When he was Chief of Staff before the Six Day War, he seized up at a crucial time and blamed it on nicotine poisoning.

Peres is a wary, quick-witted man, as hard as the floor, with a steady stream of quotable quotes. Here are a few from my notebook:

"The Middle East threat is to the oily places, not to the holy places."

"Resources are more important than geography."

"The West spends more on women's cosmetics than it does on defence."

"Iran is rich enough to support revolution as an industry."

"Hussein is a smart man. He uses PLO language and Jordanian power."

And so on.

Peres keeps a colourful portrait of Ben-Gurion over his desk, a reminder of his great days in Defence under the first Israeli Prime Minister when he virtually invented the country's aircraft industry. The problem for Peres is his image. People don't trust him: they see him as a tricky wheeler-dealer. He is not an easy man to work with.

There is a sad sense in Israel, especially among intellectuals, of "13 wasted years." A professor told me: "We are a talented, ingenious people. We should have found a way in all this time of giving Hussein his land back on reasonable terms."

Moshe Dayan is blamed for this failure, for having effectively vetoed promising chances. Golda Meir is also abused for her inflexibility. I was astonished to hear one Israeli politician, a kindly man, suddenly burst out in uncontrollable rage: "Golda's soul should be burning in Hell! She was stupid, she didn't understand."

Labour's most articulate spokesman is the former Foreign Minister, Abba Eban, who wrote a stinging reply to Dayan, his successor, in the Jerusalem Post, saying that Israel's occupation of Palestinian land "has failed both as an idea and as a reality."

Much heat — in Israel as well as the United Nations — has been provoked by the Begin Cabinet's narrow decision to open a Jewish college at Hebron on the West Bank, thereby asserting a sovereign right over the biblical Judea and Samaria.

Hebron, "City of the Fathers," figures strongly in Jewish history; I met a woman who had been dramatically saved from the Jewish pogrom there in 1929. I drove to look at the town, which lies south of Bethlehem on the road to Beersheba. Apart from an Israeli soldier on a roof-top on the way in — and an obstetrician whose sign-board proclaimed a Dublin degree — the town was overwhelming Arabic. I could well believe a journalist who told me: "It would be suicide for an Israeli to walk alone in the alleys of Hebron."

Outside Abraham's tomb there I saw a group of Arab boys calling out and laughing after a young Israeli soldier. He smiled uncertainly back, fingering his gun, not sure of the Arabic, not sure what to do — not sure, perhaps, why he was there.

The Mayor of Bethlehem, Elias Freij, is a Christian Arab of aldermanic demeanour, portly, shrewd and polite. Outside his elegant office in Manger Square, air-conditioned buses unload pilgrims at the Church of Holy Nativity. One of the buses proclaims: "Nazareth Tourist and Transport Company," while a sign on a building reads: "Bethlehem Hotels Incorporated" — both institutions filling a social need felt acutely in these parts nearly two thousand years ago..

Freij is known as a "moderate", a reliable barometer of Arab opinion on the West Bank. Moderates now talk PLO. He declares the Begin–Sadat autonomy talks "bankrupt." 'We accept the PLO as our representatives.'

The West Bank Palestinians seem content to let the PLO, the men in Beirut, make the running for them. But they can oppose the PLO — as they did when they went to greet Sadat in Israel; and there are strains within the PLO. Jordan still pays official salaries on the West Bank and Hussein keeps himself informed. There is a pull towards the PLO and a pull towards Jordan: too soon to know which will prevail.

As I left the Mayor's office I asked: "If I come back here in five years' time, will I find a Palestinian State?" Freij answered carefully: "No, but you won't see any Israeli soldiers out there either."

By road through the Jordan valley. The heavy rains have brought patches of green to the bony Judean hills. The Holy Land is in bloom: plum trees, strawberries, irises, poppies, anemones. Past the "Inn of the Good Samaritan", now a police station. The ravens that fed Elijah swoop down from the Qumran caves, where the Dead Sea scrolls were found.

A swim in the Dead Sea, the lowest point on earth. It's true what they tell you at school: you can't sink in it because of the salt, which is very bitter. You can hardly swim in it either, because your legs float to the top. The floor is a black mud that Cleopatra sent for as an early beauty treatment. The tourists smother themselves in it obscenely.

Past bedouin encampments and the odd mangy camel. Ahead of us an Israeli Volkswagen smashes into the back of an old Arab jalopy, scattering pans across the road. Peace negotiations open noisily.

Then the Jordan itself, a disappointing trickle. When Kissinger saw it he remarked: "What public relations can do for a river!"

As we head north, heavy rains obscure the Sea of Galilee. The best guide-book to these parts is the Bible, but we have to rush past. Guns everywhere. Soldiers thumbing lifts, an ice-lolly in one hand, an automatic weapon in the other.

In the Golan Heights I visit a bleak Israeli outpost in the driving rain, near the Rafid triangle where Nicholas Tomalin, the *Sunday Times* journalist, was killed by a Syrian-fired Sagger missile in the 1973 war. Our escort, Major Hillel Ashkenazy, had given him his last briefing on the day he died. Ashkenazy's nephew was also killed that day in the same battle zone. As we leave, I admire the profusion of flowers on the Golan Heights. "They're all mined," he said.

Back in Jerusalem, it is the Passover, an austere time. We attend a family *seder* and join in a reading of the Haggadah, which describes the Jews' release from bondage in Egypt. The message of the Haggadah is that God abhors slavery for all mankind. Some lines leap off the page: "You should not oppress a stranger, for you know the feelings of the stranger, having yourselves been strangers in the land of Egypt" (*Exodus* 23.9). The Jews are uncomfortably aware of the moral paradox this presents in their relations with the Palestinians.

Peres invited the Egyptian ambassador, Saad Mortada, to his family *seder*. They evidently coped with the anti-Egyptian passages. Mortada is lionised by Israeli hostesses, unlike his Jewish counterpart in Cairo, who has a hard time.

No bread can be eaten in the eight days of the Passover. It is burned in the streets. No beer. The hotel can let me have a gin but no tonic. The pool is closed. A Jewish woman sympathises: "It's not so easy being a Jew." After a week of these minor deprivations, I have a mad vision of stuffing myself with bread, washed down with tonic, then hurling myself into the swimming pool.

We escape to an oasis called "The British Pub" and eat in a Chinese restaurant called "Mandy". Intrigued by the name, I ask about Mandy. Could it be the notorious Mandy Rice-Davies? I am informed politely: "Mandy was a famous and successful lady in England."

The ultra-orthodox Jews live in Mia Sherim, a warren of narrow streets that clog the centre of Jerusalem. It is virtually a no-go area, even for Israelis. By mistake, we find ourselves lost in this quarter on the holiest of days, the Sabbath in Passover week. We are shouted at angrily by men in black hats and ringlets. We are told later that, had we rounded the next corner, our car would have been stoned.

Teddy Kollek, the Mayor of Jerusalem, fights a running battle with Mia Sherim, which has threatened to put a curse on his life if he goes ahead with plans for a new road and sports stadium nearby. Kollek, a warm expansive personality, doesn't seem to mind.

An early-morning drive round Jerusalem with the Mayor is a

rare experience. When he meets traffic he plunges down side-roads or through prohibited entrances that lead past rubble and backyards to find a way through. Startled police reverse out of his path when he darts the wrong way down a one-way street. They grin and wave: "Shalom, Teddy."

The same greeting from a little girl in pigtails in the Old City, who is clearly thrilled to see him. Arab workers rise from their tasks and shake his hand. An Arab shopkeeper rushes out and yells that the repaving of Old City streets is taking too long and driving business away. Teddy yells back in Arabic and the two men part happily.

He plainly loves the city. He seems to know every tree, every new building plot. He is hurt by the criticism of Israel's stewardship of Jerusalem, some (but not all) of it badly misinformed. He cannot visualise the city being divided again. He has plans for a Greater Jerusalem — possibly including Bethlehem — where authority could be shared. But he worries that, because of the Begin Government's policies, his work may "all go to pot."

Saul Bellow described Kollek as "Israel's most valuable political asset." He is an asset to the human race, a force of nature.

Mild culture-shock after a visit to the Dome of the Rock, where Mohammed ascended to Heaven; the El Aqsa mosque where Hussein's grandfather was murdered; and on to the Wailing Wall (which is segregated).

The Church of the Holy Sepulchre, the most sacred of Christian shrines, is a shambles, covered in builders' rubble. The Golden Gate, where the Messiah is expected to come, has been sealed up for centuries. St Stephen's Gate, where the Israeli troops broke through in 1967, is about 20 yards from Bethesda, the birthplace of the Virgin Mary. On the Via Dolorosa T-shirts are on sale: "Billion Dollar Man and Wonder Woman". Life goes on.

To open a door in Israel is to be drowned in a gale of noise, chatter, questions, analysis, gossip and jokes. How to make sense of it after 10 days? You can't. You can only listen carefully and do your best.

When I was last in the country in 1971, I was besieged everywhere by the same expectant question: Well, what do you think of Israel? The questioners were confident of the answer, proud of their achievements after the stunning victories of the Six Day War. The question is still being asked, but with less confidence now. They don't expect the same answer. Negative comments are met with a shrug: "It's not so easy being a Jew."

I met a businessman in Tel Aviv, who asked: "Are they filling you with propaganda — or telling you what it's really like here?"

"Tell me what it's really like."

"It's like I imagine South Africa is. We're going nowhere. There's nowhere to go. You take your country for granted all your life, then you travel and find there are better places. That's why people are leaving. They're depressed."

At the heart of this man's problem is the economy. Inflation is running at 140 per cent a year (some say more). Interest rates are 10 per cent a month.

The economic crisis may partly account for the mood of disenchantment in the country. The peace euphoria brought on by Sadat's historic visit has largely evaporated. Many Israelis fear Sadat has out-manoeuvred Begin and usurped Israel's special relationship with America. The wonder of going to Cairo is also wearing thin: Israelis come home complaining of poor hotels and dirty streets. But such moods are ephemeral. I may have caught them at a bad time.

To test the mood I went to the country's artists. There was an exhibition at the Israel Museum on the theme of "Borders". The images were vivid: a man's head as a map, the cease-fire lines as a dress pattern, photos of a dog marking out its territory, flowers on barbed wire.

Grim, certainly, descriptive, even matter-of-fact, compared with the stark horror of Yad Vashem, the Holocaust museum. Israel cannot be understood without the Holocaust. Everyone in the country either lost someone or survived it; just as every family in Israel has survived or lost someone in the four wars since independence. After the Holocaust museum it was unnerving to see a hotel porter with the name-tab: "George Nazi."

One emerges from Yad Vashem with a powerful sense of fundamental sickness in the human psyche. The experience has shaped Israel's attitude to the world and conditioned its relations with the Arabs, who also come in the night to kill them. It is a terrible irony that the Jews should have come together for refuge in one of the most dangerous spots on earth.

And yet, even in bad times there is an energy about Israel, a desperate will to survive, that can be found nowhere else. It is partly the sense of shared national purpose that sweeps it along; partly, perhaps, a special sense of being in the mainstream of history. "Happy the nation whose annals of history are boring to read" (Montesquieu).

Everyone you meet in Israel has an amazing personal story. I met a taxi-driver whose aunt had arrived in Israel the day before from Minsk in Russia; she hadn't seen his father for 60 years. Many of the Soviet Jews don't stay; they go on to America. But the immigrant mix seems to be working better than people feared. There are black Jews from Ethiopia. The South African and Indian Jews play cricket together.

Can Israel make the mental adjustments that will gain it acceptance in the outside world? There are problems that will have to be faced, quite apart from the atavist distrust of outsiders built into the Jewish consciousness.

Israel gave back Sinai to Egypt in return for an offer of peace; the return of the West Bank is being demanded without an offer of peace. For the return of Sinai the Israelis spoke direct to Sadat: they could look into his eyes and judge his sincerity. In the autonomy talks they also deal with Sadat, but they know that one day they will have to talk to Palestinians, maybe the PLO. Whatever they concede now to Sadat will be the starting-point for the next negotiations.

There are hopeful signs. The Jerusalem Post tells the awkward truth day after day. On West Bank settlements: "A more striking feat of irrelevance could hardly be conceived." On the PLO: "Israel can no longer ignore the fact that the Palestinian state idea has become not only respectable but by now entrenched in world opinion."

This sounds like the beginnings of a new wisdom. I found it paradoxical that Israel should be in such as disenchanted mood when, after 32 years, a genuine peace could be in sight. Perhaps, I thought, the country has embarked on a mental migration and this mood may be just part of the painful process of coming to terms with new realities. Perhaps.

Professor J. L. Talmon, of the Hebrew University, has said: "It is the fate of the Jews to serve as a testimony, as a living witness, a touchstone, a whipping block and symbol all in one." It's not so easy being a Jew.

The *Observer*, 1980

THE MAN WHO MADE MALAWI

In 1963 I went to Nyasaland (soon renamed Malawi when it became independent) to edit the country's main newspaper. I was 25. I became a correspondent in Africa for the BBC and several British newspapers, including The Observer, *which I joined in London in 1966. I wrote this profile of Dr Banda in 1985 when he came to Britain on a state visit. Sadly, Malawi has fallen apart since.*

When Dr Hastings Kamuzu Banda, the Life-President of Malawi, joins the Queen at Buckingham Palace, the rich pageantry of the occasion will have more than usual significance for the most enthusiastic royalist in Africa.

It will be the fulfilment of a lifetime's dream that began in an African mud hut in the reign of Queen Victoria. Banda's precise age is a mystery: in Malawi it is a state secret. Officially, he was born in 1906; missionary records of the time point to 1902; but his biographer, drawing on family sources, argues persuasively for 1898. Nyasaland became a British protectorate in 1891, so if Banda had been born only a few years earlier he would have pre-dated colonialism altogether.

What is known for sure about his early life is that in 1915 he was wrongly ejected from an examination by a missionary for looking over another candidate's shoulder (he was actually standing up to see the blackboard better, being exceptionally small).

Because all his hopes of higher education in Nyasaland seemed to have been shattered, the young Banda, deeply wounded, set off on foot on a personal odyssey to South Africa. He didn't tell his family, who heard nothing from him for two years and assumed he had been eaten by lions.

He emerged in Hartley, Southern Rhodesia, as a sweeper in a hospital, which may have fired him with the ambition to become a doctor. He suffered more crude racial indignities there than South Africans then were capable of (apartheid was introduced much later). He was joined by his uncle, who took him to Johannesburg, where he worked in the gold mines and saved enough money to take up a Methodist scholarship in the United States.

Banda spent 12 years in America, acquiring glittering academic qualifications in a wide range of subjects at universities in Ohio, Indiana, Chicago and Tennessee, culminating in a doctorate with the highest grades ever recorded at his medical school. One of his benefactors was the wife of the inventor of Pepsodent.

In the Deep South in the 1930s Banda saw the Ku-Klux-Klan in action and even witnessed a lynching. He became acquainted with Marcus Garvey's "Back to Africa" movement and with the writings on race of Dr W.E.B. DuBois. The man who influenced him most was the American-educated Ghanaian, Dr J.E.K. Aggrey, who preached racial partnership — that "in order to produce harmony you have to play on the white keys as well as the black."

By the late 1930s Banda was ready to return to Nyasaland as his country's first native doctor but, remarkably, his American qualifications were not regarded as sufficient for a British colony. So he enrolled as a medical student in Edinburgh, where the city's puritan conservatism suited his temperament. He became an Elder of the Church of Scotland.

His wish to return home to Nyasaland was constantly frustrated. Having obtained the right qualifications, he applied to become a medical missionary, but met resistance from the European nurses, who refused to work under an African doctor. He then applied for a post in the Nyasaland government service, for which he was accepted — but only on condition that he would agree not to mix socially with Europeans. He refused.

By now it was war-time. As a pacifist, he was drafted as a GP to Tyneside. Always a fastidious, ascetic man, he found the business of treating seamen for venereal disease and Wrens for abortions not to his taste. After the war he had a popular practice in London, with a big house in Brondesbury Park, where he was personally revered by his patients.

He attended the first pan-African congress in Manchester in 1946 with Jomo Kenyatta and Kwame Nkrumah and kept in close touch by letter and cheque-book with the burgeoning Nyasaland African Congress. When white Rhodesians, led by Roy Welensky, pressed their case for a new racial partnership, the Central African Federation, to include Nyasaland and Northern Rhodesia — "a partnership of the rider and the horse," as the Europeans put it — Banda opposed it vehemently from exile and left England in disgust for the Gold Coast, soon to be independent Ghana, in 1953.

This was the worst period of Banda's life, when he ran into debt, was condemned by the local medical authorities for an undisclosed offence, and was found to be living in sin with his receptionist from London, the wife of an English major.

All this time Banda had kept in touch with the young Nyasa politicians seeking independence from British rule, for whom this exiled doctor, who had walked barefoot to South Africa as a boy, had become a potent political legend. By 1958, they judged the time was right to invite him back. He arrived home, after an absence of 43 years, to a public acclaim that has scarcely diminished since, despite the fact that he appeared before the crowd as a Chaplinesque figure in a three-piece suit with a homburg hat and a fly-whisk, and recalled scarcely a word of the local dialect.

Anyone who heard Banda in this heady period will never forget the power of his rhetoric. His speech at the opening of the Malawi University is a collector's item. He lectured his audience for hours, many of them uncultured peasants, on the structure of the English language: the difference between transitive and intransitive verbs, common nouns and proper nouns, culminating in a powerful recitation of Churchill's war-time speeches. As someone observed, the only chapter of the grammar book he evidently hadn't mastered was the one on *précis*.

Even now his speeches range widely over political theories from Cicero onwards, but there are increasing signs of restlessness in his young and mostly illiterate audiences, who come to life again when the old man, known as "the Ngwazi", goes down into the stadium to join the tribal dancers.

After a spell in Welensky's jail in 1959, from which he was rescued by his old friend Dingle Foot, the British lawyer, Banda developed a close relationship with the Governor, Sir Glyn Jones, and together they took the country peacefully to independence as Malawi in 1964. Immediately, after that, however, Banda faced a Cabinet revolt. The young turks who had invited him back as a father-figure began to resent his pedagogic and dictatorial methods of rule.

In particular, they were embarrassed by his insistence that Malawi, as a tiny landlocked nation in the heart of Africa, had to develop good relations with Portuguese Mozambique and South Africa. There was a brief civil war and the rebels were routed. Banda imposed a ruthless grip on the country's internal politics that he has never since let up.

During the civil war in 1964, as I tried to provide some balance in the coverage of the crisis in *The Times of Malawi*, which I was then editing, Banda summoned me to his office in Zomba, poked me in the chest and roared: "Keep out of my politics, Bwana Editor!

He pressed his policy of friendship with South Africa to the point where President Vorster paid a state visit to Malawi in 1970. In return, the South Africans built Banda a spectacular new capital at Lilongwe after Britain and the World Bank had refused to sanction the expenditure. South Africa has also helped Banda with security, keeping an eye on his enemies in exile.

Malawi, relying mainly on tea, sugar and tobacco, has been one of Africa's few economic success stories. It is relatively free of corruption by African standards, though a private company originally set up by Banda has a shareholding in most new ventures.

Banda has always maintained that the way to break down racial barriers is to show white people that blacks can be as clever as they are themselves. "Look at me," he seems to be saying, "once you get to know me, you'll realise how stupid your racial theories are." ("Stupid" remains his favourite word of abuse and once used it 39 times in an attack on my newspaper). He has sometimes been heard to refer to "the Africans" as though he wasn't one himself — which is perhaps understandable in someone who spent more than half of his life outside the continent.

The Queen's guest has led one of the most remarkable lives of our time — a verdict that Banda himself would wholeheartedly endorse. The will power, beneath a disarmingly quiet manner, is prodigious. "I do things," he once said, consciously echoing Bismarck: "Let others explain." His proud puzzlement, even arrogance, about himself showed in another self-judgement: "I am not just another African. I am Kamuzu."

Banda has always been a man caught between two worlds, a would-be philosopher-king forced to use the toughest methods to bend his country to his own eccentric will. There is a sense in which Malawi will not be truly independent, nor truly African, until he goes.

The *Observer*, 1985

A WALK IN THE WOODS WITH GROMYKO

Andrei Gromyko served under seven Soviet leaders, from Stalin to Gorbachev, as Foreign Minister, Ambassador to the United States, United Nations and Britain and played a key role in arms talks. When the Observer *bought his memoirs, I asked for an interview and he agreed. I saw him at his dacha outside Moscow. I made a broadcast about the meeting for Newsnight on BBC2. He died six months later.*

TRELFORD: *You are 80 this year, the last child of the Revolution. You were a small boy in a village in Byelorussia in 1917. Do you have any recollections of that time?*

GROMYKO: Sometimes I close my eyes just before falling asleep and think of some episodes that spring up unwanted in my mind. I remember how, as a boy of five or six, we had a mare that belonged to my father, and it had a little foal. When I woke up in the morning, I saw that the foal had been eaten by the wolves. I shall never forget that.

On another occasion, a few of us had to dig into the steep bank of a river for lime. Eventually some of us gave up and went fishing instead, leaving two of my friends to go on with the digging. When we came back, we saw that the bank of the river had collapsed and our friends had been killed. Their bodies were delivered to their homes. These are my early memories, all rather unpleasant.

Were you conscious of the Revolution going on around you?

As children, we began to feel that something must be going on, because armed men kept appearing. They didn't stop in the villages but moved towards the towns. People were sympathetic towards the armed men because they had overthrown the Tsar and promised us land. Not only promised it, but actually divided up the landowners' land for the poor peasants. Unfortunately, we didn't have a single landowner in our village (which was called Old Gromyki), so we didn't get anything extra.

The conditions of life were extremely difficult. Bread was scarce, 90 per cent of the population could not make their own crop last from one harvest to the next. They had to leave the village and find seasonal jobs. Lenin's name was very well known and people were sympathetic to him. Nobody knew of Stalin then.

Why has it taken so long, 36 years, to set the historical record straight about Stalin's crimes? Are there more dark secrets to come out?

Though I met Stalin very many times, I didn't really know what was going on. The Stalin period was a period of harsh repression which carried off millions of lives. Looking back, the Party and the people began to wonder more and more why so many people had perished. Orphans, widows and relatives demanded an answer. The whole country demanded an answer.

But Stalin had one amazing quality: the ability to keep things secret. He had an entire system to conceal the facts.

Many people disappeared in the Stalin period. You survived. Did you ever come under suspicion yourself?

There was one occasion. When I was taking over our London embassy in 1952, I was working on a doctoral these on the American economy. To make my research easier, I sent a list of books and magazines in a diplomatic bag to London, addressed to myself, so that when I arrived there I could arrange for somebody to buy them for me. The books and magazines had all been recommended in an official Soviet report.

Several months later, when I was in Moscow, the Minister of Foreign Affairs, Vyshinsky, said to me: "We have received some information about you sending a certain document which you were not supposed to send. You now have to write an explanation."

"To whom?"

"To Stalin."

I was amazed by the senselessness of this suspicion.

"Do I have to?" I asked.

"Yes, you must."

"Fine, I will write it," I said.

Two or three hours later I produced a page and a half and sent if off, I stopped thinking about it. It didn't frighten me at all.

My letter must have gone to Beria, who was in charge of the secret police, and from him to Stalin. I have never heard anything about the matter since. I was absolutely calm about it at the time. Now, however, looking back in the light of all we know, I am surprised how I managed to stay so calm.

I was encouraged not to worry by an American diplomat who had been at the war-time Tehran Conference in 1943, He said that Stalin told Roosevelt: "We are pleased with our Washington ambassador, Gromyko." Perhaps that was what calmed me down. But, of course, Stalin was capable of saying one thing today and doing quite the opposite tomorrow.

You were present at those Great Power conferences that shaped the post-war world at Yalta and Potsdam. How did Stalin, Roosevelt and Churchill get on together?

Stalin preferred Roosevelt to Churchill, partly because he was more in favour of our position. He was sympathetic to Soviet claims for reparations from the Germans. Churchill said, categorically, no, no, no. Churchill was always very extreme, always took a hard line.

Stalin absolutely could not accept Churchill's view that Germany should be reborn as a single powerful country. Roosevelt was a more flexible politician, especially during conference, and Stalin liked that.

President Gorbachev is due to visit Britain very soon. Do you see any improvement in relations since the time when the Soviet Union was describing Mrs Thatcher as an Iron Lady?

Our relationship is now softer, and I have to say that Mrs Thatcher has won the favour of Soviet public opinion. For a start, she is a woman, and people like the idea of a woman as Prime Minister of an important country, our former ally. The fact that she and her Government supported the Soviet-American agreement on the liquidation of medium-and-short-range missiles made her even more popular.

At the same time, our people feel that she is too cautious about the future, that she is not sure it is worth moving resolutely towards disarmament and the liquidation of nuclear weapons. Isn't she holding too firmly to those weapons, our people ask?

Some people in the West are worried that so much is happening so fast in the Soviet Union that Mr Gorbachev may not survive and could be replaced by somebody who did not share his view on disarmament. If something happened to him — and we are all mortal — would his reforms survive him? Has he set in motion some historical process that cannot be changed?

The Soviet Union is at present crossing an historic divide. *Perestroika*, in its full revolutionary sweep, embraces all spheres of life. Gorbachev expresses the mood of the overwhelming majority of our people. *Glasnost* in itself is not enough. When you open the door, you have to have a clear view ahead about where you are trying to go.

We maintain that we have chosen the right path, we cannot afford to stand still. We are talking about standard of living, financial security, about food production and material goods. But we do not put forward deadlines. We avoid naming dates.

Just a few days ago, I talked to Gorbachev and said "Well, should we have chosen such a course and said that in three, four or five years' time we would have solved our problems? Maybe somebody in the West would have praised us for that. But that would not be serious." Gorbachev agrees. No dates. We can make some mistakes and we shall correct them.

Ligachov once seemed to imply that you had been the decisive voice in bringing Gorbachev to power. Is that true?

I have been of the firm opinion, ever since I met Gorbachev long ago, that he is a man of sharp and profound mind, with great abilities and a correct understanding of our future tasks. That is why I spoke up for him at the Central Committee plenum, when the candidate for General Secretary was being chosen.

How would you characterise Gorbachev's style?

"Dynamic" is the word I would use.

Perestroika and *glasnost* clearly run some risks. There has been trouble in the republics and resistance within the bureaucracy. Could it ever reach the point where Gorbachev's own position was threatened?

I would not like you to have the impression that our knees are shaking. Not at all. We are confident about our path and we are walking firmly. Nobody can lose out if we achieve *perestroika*. Many people will benefit from our success.

How would you compare working with Khrushchev, himself a reformer, with Brezhnev?

Khrushchev was a man of extraordinary intelligence, strong will and peasant native wit. He knew the countryside better than he knew the city. But his skills were not underpinned by a solid education. He never ran short of words. He could carry on a conversation with workers and peasants or scholars or journalists with equal, and enviable, ease. But there were some awkward moments.

During his official visit to Burma, Khrushchev went to look at the Chief Pagoda, a religious building. The gilded roof glittered in the sun. As he was leaving this Buddhist temple, he was surrounded by a number of foreign journalists, who showered him with questions. Khrushchev always like to give impromptu answers on such occasions.

To the question "How do you like the temple?" he replied: "Of course, it has a rich appearance, but then, behind all the gold there is the hard work of the ordinary Burmese people. So where is the justice in it? And not only that. The church everywhere plays a reactionary role. It was the church that burned Galileo, after all."

I tried to correct him without being noticed, by murmuring under my breath: "It wasn't Galileo, it was Giordano Bruno." But he was so carried away by this own idea that he saw no need to correct his error. But of course the journalists, whom you can't trust an inch, took note of it and many of them grinned.

Khrushchev showed great strength of will and determination after Stalin's death, when he made his speech at the Twentieth Party Congress, condemning the Stalin cult.

That is a powerful page in his biography and Khrushchev's chief contribution to Soviet history.

Why did he go so suddenly?

People talk as though he was ousted by Brezhnev in a Stalinist coup, but that is absurd. The Central Committee were unanimously of the view that Khrushchev was a spent force.

His main mistake was his decision to divide the Party into two, an industrial half and an agricultural half. It was impossible to accept.

On foreign policy issues, he could grasp the essence of a problem quickly. He was firm on disarmament.

We were flying home from Bulgaria on one occasion when he said to me: "I've come to the conclusion that we have to deploy some of our nuclear rockets in Cuba. Otherwise the Americans will invade the island despite their failure at the Bay of Pigs,"

I replied: "It will cause a political explosion in the USA. That has to be taken into account."

But he couldn't be shifted. He said: "I still intend to put this question to the Politburo very soon." And so he did. What happened after that is well-known.

Working with Khrushchev wasn't easy. He was always coming up with new ideas. Brezhnev was a different man. He uttered no fresh ideas. He admitted frankly that he was not well-informed on foreign affairs. His weakness was that he had no deep understanding of problems. He would listen intently to different opinions in the Politburo, but he had difficulty in making up his mind and things were often left hanging in the air.

It was amazing in retrospect that so many agreements were concluded at that time, including the Anti-Ballistic Missile Treaty, the Salt 1 and 2, and the Helsinki Final Act, despite Brezhnev's health and his impermissible slowness in examining many questions, including foreign policy issues.

He was an emotional man, easily moved to tears. When the news came through that Taraki, the general secretary of the Afghan Communist Party, had been brutally murdered in his study, it was too much for Brezhnev to bear. He was simply beside himself. Taraki's murder has to be taken into account when considering the steps taken by the Soviet Union in Afghanistan.

Was Afghanistan a major error?

Afghanistan is not only a friendly country but our neighbouring country. We have a very long border. The Afghan Government asked the Soviet Union 11 times for help to fight outside aggression, mainly from Pakistan.

But the Afghan leadership did not have a very clear picture of its internal potential. It overestimated its abilities and the population's readiness to accept certain social reforms. But I don't want to analyse the problem retrospectively. Better to look at the future.

What did you and Brezhnev disagree about?

Alcoholism. The doctors were reporting alarming facts on this issue. It was perfectly obvious that the last person willing to look at this problem was the General Secretary himself.

Later over dinner, I asked Gromyko if Brezhnev had a personal drink problem.

"The answer to your question," he said after a significant pause is Yes, Yes, Yes." (Gromyko himself gave up drinking after an incident as a small boy, when he and a friend were very ill after finding some bootleg liquor and drinking it.) Gromyko continued: "I raised the matter with Brezhnev in these words: 'Socialism and the boozing of vodka by the people don't go together. Why is the Politburo silent on this?' He heard me out patiently and then said: "The Russians have always drunk vodka. They can't get by without it." He wouldn't agree to any further discussion. He particularly emphasised the words: "They can't get by without it."'

The question was properly debated under Gorbachev, who tabled it with force and conviction. Perestroika and drunkenness are diametrical opposites and the country as a whole understands this.

What kind of leader would Andropov have made?

I always had the highest opinion of Andropov, who was a friend. We tended to agree on things and sometimes worked together to convince Brezhnev of something. Regrettably, over many years Andropov became more and more seriously ill.

A personal question. Your face is known throughout the West for its impassivity. Like a poker player, you give nothing away. Yet I can see you are a very human person. What are you interested in?

I am a great lover of books — Tolstoy, Pushkin, Gogol, Lermontov. And, of course, Shakespeare, Goethe, Sir Walter Scott. I am also a good swimmer. I have learned how to swim in the water like a fish.

The *Observer*, 1989

BRAVE SOULS OF EUROPE

This article is an abridged version of a lecture I gave at the English Speaking Union

Nobody predicted the astonishing collapse of the Communist empire — not politicians, think-tanks, diplomats or journalists.

If the system collapsed so quickly, how had it lasted so long? The answer is Soviet power, which — through an astonishing act of will that lasted 45 years — created in the Iron Curtain one of the most artificial structures in history, one that also suited the West's convenience because it brought relative stability after years of war.

Western Europe huddled together and achieved a prosperity undreamt of in the rubble of World War Two. Germany was divided and tamed. Troublesome ghosts like Transylvania, Macedonia, Serbia — now loose again — were consigned to history.

To see the liberation of Eastern Europe as having been caused only by the failure of the Marxist system, however — as the ultimate triumph of capitalism — is too complacent a response. It was essentially a long-delayed process of decolonisation. Like the British and French empires of the past, the Kremlin had to learn the limits of its power.

The humiliation in Afghanistan was an important part of this process. It strengthened Gorbachev's hand against the old guard, since he had opposed the intervention; it revealed the military and KGB as incompetents; it released back into Soviet society, as with the Americans in Vietnam, a young class of rebellious, armed and often drug-addicted ex-soldiers; it demonstrated that Stalin's heirs had neither the will nor the resources for foreign adventures.

The effect of this in Eastern Europe was crucial, for it became clear that the corrupt old Communist Party leaders could no longer rely on the Red Army to crush opposition, which gave heart to the democratic forces ranged against them.

Having fired the engine, Gorbachev could not apply the brakes, so the train clattered on and hasn't stopped rolling yet. Whether Gorbachev himself will be found in the wreckage remains to be seen. In a sense he has already failed, for his main aim was to preserve what power he could for the Soviet Communist Party, which now has no power at all.

The Soviet economy is in a free fall. Currency, bank debts, budget deficits, statistics, the whole infrastructure and environment, are disaster areas. They are starting from almost nothing — possibly less than nothing if inflation goes on rising tenfold every year.

There is little understanding of what a market system requires. People like Hungarians and Czechs, especially the former East Germans, had some acquaintance with a capitalist or mixed economy: it existed in living memory in their country or just across the border in the West.

People in the Soviet Union have known nothing but Communism for three generations, and centuries of feudalism before that. One of President Bush's aides explained the attitude problem this has created: "The Russians have no experience of living with envy. They've never lived in a society where it's OK to earn more than somebody else."

A US Treasury figure said he'd been to Albania and heard their plans for economic reform, which sounded fine on paper. Then one of the leaders, a reformed old Communist, took him aside and said: "But how can we eliminate speculation?" The American had to explain that speculation was now the name of the game.

As the Third World has found to its cost, you can swap one master for another and still remain slaves. In Europe the Iron Curtain is being replaced by a Poverty Curtain, or at least for the more southern of the former Soviet satellites. Hungary, Poland, Czechoslovakia may in time be welcomed aboard the Euro-gravy train, but nobody is eager to embrace Albania.

One scenario, which turns East Europe into a new Taiwan or Hong Kong by producing cheap manufacture goods for the West with a high-skill, low-wage workforce, strikes me as over-optimistic.

How should the West respond to all this? The first test is military security. Brent Scowcroft, Bush's National Security Adviser, said recently: "We have no experience of a disintegrating super-power which has 27,000 nuclear warheads. It behoves us to be careful". One can hardly argue with that.

Nonetheless, President Bush's bold unilateral cuts in America's nuclear forces — and the qualified reciprocal promise yesterday by Mr Gorbachev — give grounds for hope that the way will soon be clear for a comprehensive arms agreement that must be an indispensable precondition for serious aid to the Soviet economy. The US is entitled to see immediate results on the ground, including the removal of all land-based tactical nuclear weapons from Europe.

It is surely a good bargain for both sides if guns can be exchanged for butter while the shadow of nuclear war — at least between the US and the Soviet Union — is finally banished from the earth.

In Washington I found support for emergency aid over the coming winter to meet the expected Soviet shortages in food, medicine, fuel and housing. But I did not find any commitment to a long-term Marshall aid programme beyond that; not yet, anyway.

There were practical reasons for this: continuing violence in the republics, the lack of private property rights or a constitutional basis in law for contracts to protect private investors.

But there were also philosophical reservations. One State Department official put it like this: "Why did the Soviet empire fail? Because Marxism didn't work?" OK, but what if it wasn't as simple as that? Maybe the Soviet empire died like other empires of the past, because it took on political and military commitments way beyond its means, so that its own people finally revolted.

"This could happen to us in the next century, especially if we take on the Soviet Union and East Europe on top of our other global commitments — when our own cities are imploding with violent crime, drugs and racial tension."

This apocalyptic view, otherwise known as the doctrine of America First, is one we are likely to hear more about in the coming election years. What it amounts to in practice is not neo-isolationism, but a new and more careful assessment of where America's real interest lie. The old Manichean divide between Communist enemies and anti-Communist friends is over.

The US will not act as the world's policeman except where vital American interests are seen to be at risk. They were at risk in the Gulf, but not in Yugoslavia, and certainly not in Africa.

Nonetheless, as the Bush administration knows very well, the US does have a powerful vested interest in rebuilding the economies and societies of Eastern Europe. Jeane Kirkpatrick put it succinctly: "Whatever it costs it will be cheaper than fighting another war".

But it shouldn't all be left to US: the EC and Japan have responsibilities too — for developing trade as well as aid. It makes obvious sense to wind down Europe's common agricultural policy to allow food imports from the East.

The EC has provided Eastern Europe with an enticing example of prosperity, liberty, social welfare, and quality of life, Yet the founding fathers started it, not for economic reasons alone, but to achieve the political stability and inter-dependence on the continent that would avoid future wars. It is time now to extend that vision to the whole of Europe.

As Vaclav Havel put it: "The West cannot be indifferent to the fate of the East as a matter of principle, but it cannot be indifferent for practical reasons either."

Havel is a reminder of the remarkable personal courage and idealism that swept away evil forces which had over-shadowed a large part of the earth for most of this century. The light thus lit in Europe should not be allowed to go out. We would be failing the brave souls who achieved this miracle — and ultimately failing ourselves — if we showed any less courage and idealism in the way we respond.

The *Observer*, 1991

Night Train to Moscow

You could barely miss her — a tall blonde with hair trailing down to the back of her knees, trousers tucked into high-heeled boots. She would stand out anywhere — but in the gloom at Leningrad Station she made a striking contrast with the middle-aged, grey-haired men with their little suitcases, waiting wearily, like me, for the midnight train to Moscow.

She was talking earnestly to a chap, but it was hard to gauge from the tenor of their conversation whether they were engaged in a tearful farewell, a lovers' tiff or a hastily negotiated pick-up. Before I could form a view about this, or even work out what language they were using, the lights in the train had come on and old women were standing like soldiers outside each door to collect our tickets.

"Number 10," said the babushka, pointing vaguely inside. I struggled with the Cyrillic script, sorted out what seemed to be the right compartment, and pulled back the door. There they stood — the blonde and the chap — talking as earnestly as ever, startled now by my interruption. I was surprised to see that, instead of the expected bunks, there were two single beds about 18 inches apart. Thinking I had stumbled into the wrong place, I made my excuses and left.

"Not 10," I said, showing the babushka my ticket. "Not 10? Yes, 10!" she replied firmly, and led me back down the corridor. She pulled open the door, banged on one of the beds and ordered: "You sleep here, now!" I meekly did as I was told, kicked off my shoes, hung up my jacket, lay on the bed and picked up my Kingsley Amis novel. Peeping out now and then from behind the book, I watched with some interest as the babushka tore into the couple in heated Russian.

After a while the blonde turned to me and, seeing me reading an English novel, addressed me haltingly in that tongue: "I'm sorry," she said. "this man, he is a Finn. I meet him two years ago on holiday in Soche. Tonight we meet by accident at Hotel Astoria in Leningrad; I am leaving, he is arriving. He insist he buy me champagne; he insist he bring me to station; he insist he travel with me to Moscow. But I tell him, 'impossible', he has no ticket, he has no visa. But he is a Finn, he is therefore drunk. I am sorry. This is the problem."

Before I could reply, the drunken Finn turned on me suspiciously and started poking me in the ribs. "You," he said aggressively, "you arrange this. She is your girl-friend. You sleep with her to Moscow!" "No, no, you've got the wrong end of the stick there, old chap," I said placatingly into his bleary, uncomprehending eyes.

By this time the compartment had started filling up, as various grades of railway official offered their advice. The raised voices had attracted a crowd of fellow-travellers outside, who stood around in their socks and braces wondering what was going on. They were grinning, and I suddenly saw how the situation looked to them: Here was a beautiful Russian girl being fought over by two foreigners, one British, the other a Finn. Who was going to win?

Faces went sterner as the besotted and desperate Finn started scattering roubles around. Eventually the police arrived and the poor fellow was marched off up the platform, doubtless to some overcrowded gulag reserved for drunken Finns in Leningrad. Doors banged, whistles blew and there I was — stuck in the railway compartment alone with the blonde.

Gentlemanly, I asked if she'd like me to find another compartment. "Not necessary. They won't allow. This is usual in Soviet Union. Not to worry. Nyet problem," she replied, We introduced ourselves. She turned out to be Olga, a 29-year-old divorced paediatrician from Moscow.

"What happens now?", I asked naively. "Soon they will bring us tea," she said. "When the tea is finished, the radio goes off, the lights go half off, you get undressed. When the lights go completely off, we go sleep." So: the tea came, the tea went, the radio went off, the lights went half off, and we started to undress. By this time the train was on the move through the white night and lurching round corners, so we kept bumping into each other and laughing. Gentlemanly again, I said I'd go and clean my teeth and undress in the bathroom while she got ready for bed.

As I came out of the bathroom, with my clothes and shoes clutched in my arms, all the lights on the train suddenly went out. I staggered along the corridor seeking number 10 in the darkness. I pulled open a door and fell in — right on top of a bald old Russian who scrambled awake and hurled me back into the corridor, my clothes scattered all over the place. I finally found what must now be known as "our" compartment, where she was rolling around with laughter at my antics along the corridor.

"I can just imagine the dilemma," said Clive James afterwards. "You lie there thinking: what if she's a KGB agent? The moment you go near she'll press a buzzer and the guards will come charging in, the lights blazing and cameras whirring. On the other hand, maybe she isn't... maybe it's your birthday."

"You didn't, of course," say my male friends sternly. "You wouldn't take such a risk. You wouldn't be such as fool."

"I bet you did," say most of the women I know.

I was in the Soviet Union to help Garry Kasparov, the world chess champion, write his book. When I told him the story he beseeched me: "Come on, Donald, you must tell. What happened?" Hating to disappoint either romantics or realists I said what I say to all such inquiries "It's like President Reagan over Irangate (a big story at the time): "I really don't remember."

Besides, as my elder daughter put it so charmingly: "Why should a beautiful intelligent Russian woman give *you* a second glance?"

The *Illustrated London News*, 1987

6 | PAPER TIGERS

When Harry met Rupert

The trouble with Harry is that he lost his job and it happened to be the best job in the world (except, of course, for mine). Editing the *Times* may be less glamorous or rewarding than reading an autocue for ITN or being, say, lead singer for the Screaming Nobodies, but it has its own special attractions if you like that kind of thing. Or, as Malcolm Muggeridge was fond of saying, it's better than working.

One of the lesser attractions of the job is that Rupert Murdoch thinks he could do it better himself, which may or may not be true. Whether it is true or not, however, he'll have your balls for breakfast. An unfortunate side-effect of reading a revenge drama like this (*Good Times, Bad Times*, Weidenfeld & Nicolson) is that you find yourself using phrases like that.

If the editor of the *Times* can address his predecessor, albeit in a trying moment, with "You little fucker, I'll come in there and wring your neck", what hope is there for the rest of us, let alone the English language? It seems incredible that only two-and-a-half years before Philip Howard felt able to describe *Times* editors as "reverend signors grave with the knowledge that, if the world were run from Printing House Square, it would be a saner place". It is a measure of Mr Murdoch's stewardship that such as remark — probably half-serious when it was uttered — looks ludicrous today.

Fleet Street's historic successes have tended to come in pairs: Beaverbrook and Christiansen, King and Cudlipp, Thomson and Hamilton, Murdoch and Lamb, Rothermere and English — one mainly a commercial talent, the other a journalist. The weighting in each case was different, but the outcome was similar — a newspaper that knew its own market and how to reach it. Evans and Murdoch were never likely to be a successful double-act in this sense because they were facing different ways. Evans's book invites us to choose between them — a choice he presents as a stark one between Good and Evil.

If one finally resists that choice it is because neither emerges as perfectly suited to the *Times*. For all their quarrels, Harry and Rupert had too much in common. Both could cry out with Northcliffe in Max Beerbohm's cartoon: "Help! Again I feel the demons of sensationalism rising within me!" Both are intensely competitive men, in small things as well as large ones. Both have a chip; both make things fizz; neither stays to pick up the pieces.

Most people affected by the drama would agree with Evans about "the atmosphere of intrigue, fear and spite" at Murdoch's *Times*, but they might share out the blame in different proportions. It was undoubtedly Murdoch's brooding, jet-lagged restlessness that set the mood, but Evans made a basic mistake in failing to hold the journalists together. Also, the *Times* was costing a fortune and a paper that is losing money is never completely free.

Meanwhile, as they fought over the scalpel the patient lay whimpering on the operating table. The dramatic events described in this book can only be understood against the background of industrial agony and acute personal strain in which Times Newspapers found themselves at the end of 1980. The Murdoch takeover followed two years of blood-letting at Printing House Square, including 11 months of non-publication and losses of £30 million.

It is no wonder, then, that Murdoch moved in with such ease. Resistance was low: management was exhausted, bruised and resentful; the unions even more so. Murdoch was chosen because an Exocet was thought to be needed, and he could be relied on to be tough (tough with printers, that is; being tough with editors was not what the Thomson family had in mind when they entrusted their papers to him).

When, over lunch at the Savoy Grill, Murdoch persuaded him to move to the *Times*, Harold Evans was 52, at the peak of his career. He had edited the *Sunday Times* successfully for 14 years. His campaigns to compensate the victims of thalidomide and to publish the Crossman Diaries had been acclaimed at home and abroad. His stock was so high that, in retrospect, he should have stayed where he was and fought Murdoch on the firm ground he knew, rather than on the shifting sands down the road — a verdict, one suspects he might privately acknowledge.

Even if the engine-driver's son could not resist the kudos of the *Times* for ever, he might at least have stayed put for Murdoch's initial blitzkrieg — and then, ironically, he might have had the satisfaction of succeeding Charles Douglas-Home there, rather than vice versa.

It is always easy to say where other newspapers went wrong, especially afterwards. For example, the *Sunday Times* should never have merged with the *Times* in 1966; the Thomson group should have learned that lesson and sold the titles separately in 1981; they should not have trusted Murdoch enough to offer him both papers when he already owned the *Sun* and the *News of the World;* and someone (Sir Denis Hamilton? Evans himself?), should have spoken up louder against it; in any event, the Government should never have allowed it to happen.

Evans makes these points convincingly. If he is less convincing about his own role at key moments, it isn't for lack of candour. He is such an engaging, honest fellow that his faults, as well as his virtues, shine clearly through the book, and he makes no attempt to conceal them. It is much the raciest newspaper narrative since Hugh Cudlipp's 20 years ago: rich in flavour, anecdote and personality, though unbalanced in construction, somewhere between an autobiography, a parade of his triumphs, and an Insight report on his year at the *Times*. The frenzy of those final days is captured with a verve, speed and economy that Insight would do well to emulate. Even the faintly discernible whine of self-pity seems fully justified.

The portrait of Gerald Long, the former chief executive of Times Newspapers, is a classic: "Most of the time he was a man on horse-back: whip in hand, ramrod back, chin out, aglow in the morning air and ready for anything. Laughter was more frequent than anger, though both alarmingly began in the same way: head back and roaring. One did not know whether to grin or duck. Occasionally the rider vanished, leaving a set of rumpled clothing barely animated by a tired old man."

But the man who stalks through this book — or rather "slouches, leading with a shoulder, dragging a foot", with his deep frown and heavy jowls — is Rupert Murdoch himself: the author even makes him look like Richard Nixon.

One of the most moving moments in the book is the Soliloquy of St James's Square, where Evans walks around in anguish trying to decide whether he can summon the strength for a campaign to fight Murdoch off. This was the crucial decision, but he was making it too late: he should have taken Bernard Donoughue's advice and faced that choice before "the vivid rascal" (Mrs Evans's first impression of Murdoch) came to captivate him, as he has captivated so many otherwise sensible men. Instead of that, he was busy trying to set up a rival consortium to buy the *Sunday Times*, competing with (and losing to) Murdoch in tycoonery, and thereby starting at a disadvantage.

For all his tactical errors, though, Harold Evans holds an important place in the history of the *Times*. He forced "the black friars of Printing House Square" (Northcliffe's phrase) to accept the idea of change and thereby cleared a path for his successors. As for his fight for editorial freedom, I am naturally prejudiced in his favour. It was an historic fight and an heroic ordeal — a far cry from the ethos evoked by his wife's new book. *Life as a Party*.

A former *Times* editor, Sir William Haley said in his farewell address to the staff: "There are things which are bad and false and ugly, and no amount of specious casuistry will make them good or true or beautiful." That is roughly what another former *Times* editor is saying here about the man who controls more of our newspapers than anyone else in history.

The *Listener*, 1983

PRINCESS HORSEWHIPS THE PRESS

This article, written 34 years ago, shows that the battle between the Royal family and the tabloids, as shown in the cases of Prince Harry and Prince Andrew, is nothing new.

When Princess Anne rose to attack the Press at Middle Temple Hall, the man sitting straight across the table — in her direct line of fire, so to speak — happened to be Rupert Murdoch. No wonder the multi-media mega-magnate looked a trifle bemused behind his curiously large new spectacles.

He wasn't the only one. For, as the assembled editors were heard to mutter afterwards, Princess Anne is the last of the royals who could reasonably complain about the attentions of the Press. Princess Diana, the Duchess of York, even Princess Michael perhaps — but not, surely not, the intrepid lady jockey and Third World Florence Nightingale. Only this week she appeared on several front pages visiting a Birmingham prison.

It wasn't always so. Indeed, it seems only a short time since she was known as the most toffee-nosed of the royals. "Princess Sourpuss," a title she inherited from her aunt, Princess Margaret. This newspaper can claim some modest credit for changing that.

It came about in 1980, in answer to a simple question by Kenneth Harris: "If you were able to change places with a commoner for a single day, with whom would you like to change places and why?" Her answer was surprising: "At this present time in my life, if I really had to make a go of something in particular, perhaps the thing I might do best is be a long-distance lorry-driver. I think I could manage that quite well." This remark was naturally taken up by the other papers and transformed her public image.

So what is she complaining about? "I have suffered severe aggravation from the amount of unadulterated trivia, rubbish and gratuitous troublemaking." This had, she admitted, given her "a rather jaundiced and cynical view of the media." She hinted at even worse, unmentionable sins by the Press: "There are a great many things I would like to say but I haven't got either the time or the guts."

If Princess Anne was referring to various stories about her own marriage, then many journalists would accept that these were indefensible. But she cast her net wider: "I would like to be able to read a newspaper or magazine, or watch the news on television, without having to make constant translations and adjustments for exaggeration and bias." She referred, in particular, to the handling of stories about drugs, kidnaps, the Falklands and famine in Africa.

What the Princess's attack amounted to, as I understood it, was something like this: if the Press can be so wrong, so trivial and so irresponsible about the Royal Family, the subject I know most about, then they may be wrong, trivial, irresponsible, etc. about everything else. This doesn't follow, of course, but perhaps it's time that somebody said it.

The press has certainly given the Royal Family a basinful of codswallop, as the tabloids might put it, over recent months, and it was this, I suspect, that fired Princess Anne's remarks. Constant speculation about Princess Diana's "condition" must be tiresome and intrusive ('Diana the Dictator,' 'Slim Craze is Hitting Di's Bid for New Baby'). Sarah Ferguson has also had a fair sprinkling of garbage ('Fergie's Secret Naughty Nibble,' 'Fergie in Tears after Bust-Up over Koo,' etc.). There was a vicious non-story ('I snorted coke in Palace Loo') about Princess Margaret and a phantom drug-pusher. 'Twenty Things You Didn't Know about Prince Charles's Bald Spot' are about 20 more than anybody wants or needs to know.

The Royal Family understands well enough that most of the stories written about them are positive and favourable. They also know that the people's perception of them is created far more by seeing them on television than by tittle-tattle in the tabloids. Their popularity has never been higher. There is no newspaper today — and no political party represented in Parliament — which supports republicanism even as a long-term objective.

And there's nothing new about the clap-trap, after all. King George VI is said to have kept a scrapbook called "Things My Daughters Never Did." So why all this fuss now?

The answer, I suspect, is that the Royal soap opera has now reached such a pitch of public interest that the boundary between fact and fiction has long been lost sight of by papers in cut-throat circulation wars. As Michael Shea, the Queen's embattled Press secretary, put it: "They are playing a circulation war game, and they will exaggerate as much as they can in order to inflate their stories on the front page."

It is not just that some papers don't check their facts or accept denials: they don't really care if the stories are true or not. Because the Royal Family doesn't normally answer back, they assume they can get away with anything.

What seems to be happening now is that the royals, especially the younger ones, are beginning to challenge that assumption. Not, as in the past, by crudely turning hoses on photographers (Prince Philip and later Prince Andrew) or telling reporters to "naff off" (Princess Anne), but by snapping back at editors themselves.

This process began in 1981 when the Queen told the then editor of the *News of the World*:'What a pompous man you are!' which resulted in Murdoch sacking him. It continued when Princess Diana indignantly berated a former editor of the *Daily Express* for suggesting that she didn't get on with Princess Anne and had caused the Prince of Wales's private secretary to resign. The Prince of Wales himself attacked the Press for "erroneous, inaccurate and exaggerated reporting."

Now it's Princess Anne's turn with the horsewhip — and I hope she feels better for it. Whether her lash had any effect on Mr Murdoch was hard to tell. Somehow I doubt it — I hear the fellow's a closet republican.

The *Observer*, 1986

AN EVIL MAN REMEMBERED

When news of Lord Beaverbrook's death reached the Old Vic on June 9th 1964, Binkie Beaumont, the impresario, stood up in the stalls and shouted, in the hearing of the critics Bernard Levin and Alan Brien, a single word: "Hurrah'" A few days later, a Fleet Street editor declared with calculated bitterness: "The only good reason I could think of for attending Lord Beaverbrook's funeral would be to make absolutely sure that he was dead."

Yet here we are, 20 years on, with this work of pious remembrance in which the central figure appears to some, as the editor, Logan Gourlay, puts it, "at least as charming and benevolent as the Father Christmases who wink at the world on glossy wrapping paper". Can it really be, as one of Beaverbrook's closest friends said, that "everything that anyone said about Max is true — the best things and the worst things"?

To be fair, the worst as well as the best things about the old monster are recorded in this collection of 'Maxanecdotes', as Lady Diana Cooper once called them. All but three of the 34 contributors to this book (*The Beaverbrook I Knew,* Quartet) worked for the old man in one way or another — and on page 114, James Cameron says: "I do not think anyone got to know Beaverbrook by working with him." If Cameron is right, then the book is a waste of everyone's time and effort, including his own. There is another own goal in Christopher Dobson's shrewd observations that "most of those who have written about this extraordinary man have been overawed by their subject, able only to produce cameos of their own roles in his life and revealing more about themselves than the elusive essence of Max." That certainly applies to some of the essayists here.

Even so, I still found the collection both entertaining and rewarding. This is not only because of his historic importance as the strongest influence on the British press in the second quarter of the century (Northcliffe in the first quarter, Roy Thomson in the third, Rupert Murdoch in the fourth?), which means that he repays this degree of attention, if only as a point of comparison. It is more that his outsize personality begins to take over and returns time after time, like a ghost, to haunt his own banquet. One can hardly fail to become fascinated by a man variously identified in this book as Puck, Caliban, Mephistopheles, Beelzebub, Dracula, Svengali, Iago and Faust. (Hugh Kingsmill's 'Robin Badfellow' sounds about right).

There is general agreement on Beaverbrook's physical, if not his moral peculiarities. "A most affable goblin", "an impish frog", "a strange attractive gnome", a "Hallowe'en pumpkin face" — these are the most flattering descriptions. Vicky saw him as a "compact rodent" and Cecil King as "a hideous little man with a curious face." "His mouth," said Charles Douglas-Home, "was all of him'" Hugh Cudlipp says it was "so broad that it seemed to reach his ear on each side, like a melon chopped but not severed by a machete." (All this, remember, about a legendary womaniser who, according to an actress who claimed he was her best lover since Little Tich, gave a great whoop of laughter every time).

Douglas-Home recalls him as tinier, Tom Hutchinson as taller, than expected. His voice is a rasp or a burr, his eyes "like laser beams", his hand "as silky and slithery as parchment", his memory "like a mouse-trap". Hugh Cudlipp likens him to Edward G. Robinson in Little Caesar. He appears to have received his staff in the nude more often than is usual among Fleet Street proprietors. More than one employee still recalled with awe, 20 years after his death, the loud noises the boss made in the loo.

Those who regarded his influence as malign, such as Ernest Bevin, Lord Reith, Malcolm Muggeridge and Evelyn Waugh, were not those who knew him best, though Cecil King's conclusion is worth heeding: "Beaverbrook's claim to fame lies in the fact that he was the first evil man to figure in British public life for a very long time." King, like others, took exception to Beaverbrook's habit of "humiliating and corrupting young men" or as Barbara Cartland put it, "sucking a person dry, like an orange, and then chucking him aside". The oranges, on the evidence of this book, didn't seem to mind. In fact, Beverley Baxter declares: "'I have never met anything finer or cleaner than his zeal for youth, his delight in taking a younger man and giving him a chance for a successful career." He seems to have inspired love and hate in almost equal proportions.

In seeking "the elusive essence of Max", Tom Driberg plumps for a driving restlessness and "an insatiable, wide-ranging curiosity", Hugh Cudlipp for a non-divine "rage", Michael Foot for his humour ("a volcano of laughter") and "the sacred gift of enthusiasm, Hazlitt's gusto". Alan Watkins, still seething at the memory of having to assemble a parcel of honey, coffee and cider vinegar to be sent to Beaverbrook in the West Indies (not, admittedly, the best use of his talents), suggests his "love of mischief."

A.J.P. Taylor, who personally rescued Beaverbrook's reputation as a serious historian with one review in the *Observer* that likened him to Tacitus, sees at the root of the man "uncertainty and a craving for affection." Christopher Dobson writes: "He could charm people into doing what he wanted, and if charm failed he used money or fear."

Everyone agrees about his unusual vitality, zest and *joie de vivre,* which spilled over into the *Daily Express* and buoyed it up with optimism and surprise. Everyone agrees also that he was a great newspaperman, though he rarely set foot in Fleet Street after the 1920s. Barbara Cartland says he taught her to write, and Lord Blake acknowledges Beaverbrook's "excellent advice" on writing history. His editors still reel from the torrent of memos (147 instructions in a single day) that poured out of his telephone and dictaphone from all corners of the globe at the rate of 400 words a minute. Bob Edwards, who received hundreds of these on his desk as editor of the *Daily Express,* writes: "They don't make them like that any more. It's probably a good thing really. The best thing to do was to fasten your seatbelt and enjoy the ride."

And yet, according to Lord Blake, Beaverbrook himself declared that it was "essential to leave editors with complete freedom and never interfere." One one occasion, he recalls, this was the theme of a lunch at Cherkley. "I entirely agree,' said Brendan Bracken. "I never interfere in the *Financial Times*." Then news came of a Cabinet crisis and both men spent hours on the telephone instructing their staff how to handle the story. "When they had finished," says Blake, "they resumed their discussion of editorial freedom as if nothing at all had happened."

As a guide to Beaverbrook's importance this sort of book clearly has its limitations. Most of the witnesses are journalists, which means that the political side of his life is barely covered (except in one telling and dismissive remark by David Farrer, his former political secretary: "His advice was usually wrong and his interventions unfailingly ill-chosen.") The risk of anecdotal evidence, some of it second-hand, is of embellishing the legend without revealing the man.

Alan Brien has a point, though, when he says that Beaverbrook was exactly the kind of man who comes alive best, not in the letters and documents he left behind (his family burned a mysterious great heap of these, at his request, while he lay on his death-bed) but in the tales of his hired hench-persons." He lives on in El Vino, the Cheshire Cheese, the Garrick Club and other drinking-holes with a vivid presence that will not be found in Whitehall or the City. As another contributor says: "Beaverbrook needed a Boswell, but it is too late now." In Boswell's absence, this will have to do.

The *Listener,* 1984

FLEET STREET ON STAGE

In 1985 the ethics and conduct of newspapers were a major issue, prompted by the supposed influence of owners like Rupert Murdoch and Robert Maxwell. This was the focus of a play, Pravda, at the National Theatre. I took part in a stage performance before the play with the authors. This article incorporates the remarks I made then.

At one point in Pravda, the play at the National Theatre by David Hare and Howard Brenton, a newspaper owner, Lambert Le Roux, asks a serious question of a drama critic, who happens to be lying drunk on the floor at the time. This reminded me of my only visit to the offices of the real-life Pravda in Moscow, when I had to step over the body of a drunken man to get into the building. It must have been their drama critic.

Le Roux's question is a good one and deserves a better response than the alcoholic burp and black-out it gets in the play. His question is: "What sort of criteria do you use in your reviews? Is it more important that the play flatters your personal prejudices, or do you make a genuine attempt at objectivity?"

No one could say that the authors of Pravda set out to flatter the prejudices of anyone, such as myself, professionally engaged in Fleet Street. By my count our trade is convicted of the following vices: ambition, cruelty, cynicism, incompetence, complacency, defeatism, snobbery, bias, deception, plagiarism, triviality, sycophancy (to politicians as well as to owners), cowardice, corruption, of being opinionated, arrogant and drunk, of lacking convictions, of having fantasies about our own power and influence, and no solidarity.

To set against this catalogue of sins, what virtues can we offer? The authors allow us hardly any — a sentimental attachment to the rituals of the game (the noise of the presses, the bustle of deadlines, that sort of thing), just a faint spark of rebellious idealism in one character, perhaps, which is soon snuffed or charmed out of him. Then there's Rebecca, the so-called "graduate in investigative journalism" and the chosen voice of conscience in the play: what is her solution? All she can suggest to her editor-husband is that he should assert his integrity by getting out of "this filthy profession."

There is much in Fleet Street that deserves to be parodied. Some stories are inventions, some stories are loaded with political bias, some campaigns are launched (and some editorial opinions manipulated) to promote the owner's commercial interests. No one in Fleet Street can seriously deny these charges.

One of Le Roux's teasing gibes about newspapers — "Why go to the trouble of producing good ones, when bad ones are so much easier? And they sell better too" — might be taken as a rationale (or epitaph) for much of our tabloid press. Another strikes at the heart of all jaded liberals: "In England you can never fight because you do not know what you believe...Editorial freedom? You never used it when you had it."

Pravda holds up a mirror to Fleet Street all right — and if the image seems distorted in some ways, we have only ourselves to blame. But the mirror does distort, none the less. It is an insult to many good journalists to say that they are unwilling to fight to preserve their independence under fire. In my experience, there are plenty of journalists with guts and convictions who are prepared to stand up and be counted. Not all proprietors seek to impose their opinions.

And not all newspaper directors crumble like the ones shown in the play.

Even on those papers where there are heavy-handed proprietors (and I'm told there are some like that) only a small number of journalists are likely to be involved. The rest go about their normal business of informing and entertaining without a thought for the battles around the editor's chair. It makes little difference to at least 80 per cent of a newspaper's service who actually owns it.

My main reservation about the play is not that it is rude to journalists, but that it places too much weight on the supposed malign influence of proprietors as the source of all our ills. I can see why it was tempting to do this: the figure of Lambert Le Roux is a magnificent, monstrous creation and powerfully presented on stage by Anthony Hopkins. But there is a danger that the blame for Fleet Street's problems will be too conveniently directed at such demon figures, because they are easy targets and intrinsically fascinating characters, rather than at the system which brought them about.

There are two more basic reasons for the situation Fleet Street finds itself in than the alleged power mania of proprietors or the weakness and follies of journalists. One (a prosaic one in this context) is the inflated cost of producing Fleet Street papers, which makes it hard to attract normal commercial investors prepared to run them in a normal hands-off commercial manner. Benevolent newspaper owners like the Astors and the Thomsons didn't get out because they wanted to buy stud farms, like an owner in the play, but mainly because they were driven out by uneconomic printing arrangements.

The other reason (scarcely touched on in the play) is even more relevant to the capacity of newspapers to tell the truth, to let people know what is really happening in the country. This is the endemic secrecy of our society, in which access to official information is tightly controlled and parcelled out in small bits to the favoured few at times that suit the person giving it. It is a subtly corrupting system and the missing link in our democracy.

Things got worse rather than better under Margaret Thatcher, despite her proclaimed radical wish, echoed by Lambert le Roux, to "make people see their real situation." No government trusts the people enough to let them see "life as it really is." The main difference between her government and its predecessors, as far as the Press is concerned, is that it goes out of its way to reward those journalists it regards as helpful, while harassing its critics. Knighthoods and private briefings for the favourites, the threat of policemen's boots for the rest.

As for finding things out, it is true that some of our newspapers have already given up the attempt and settled instead for a purely entertainment function, featuring competitions, nudity and fictional soap operas. The question is: does that really matter if it is what people want to read?

I believe is does matter. It matters because the press matters. Pravda seems to be saying something far more negative, much more anarchic. If I read the play aright, its central message is: "This is what the press is really like, behind all the show-off and the posturing. It takes itself too seriously. Ignore it. It has no God-given role in our society. It's just a joke, another symptom of what's gone wrong with Britain". There is no attempt at discrimination, no offer of any solution.

Yet the press, as Tom Stoppard has said, has "a vital, dignified and responsible function to perform in any society that really claims to be free". A character in one of his plays puts the point precisely: "No matter how imperfect things are. If you've got a free press everything is correctable, and without it everything is concealable."

To which, admittedly, another character replies: "I'm with you on the free press: it's the newspapers I can't stand.

Clearly Messrs Brenton and Hare can't stand the newspapers either. If so, may I remind them of another positive sentiment in the Stoppard play which I don't find in theirs. At the end a much-travelled photographer concludes: "I've been around a lot of places. People do awful things to one another. But it's worse in places where everybody is kept in the dark. It really is. Information is light. Information, in itself, about anything, is light. That's all you can say, really."

The *Observer*, 1985

THE JOURNALIST AS PATRIOT

When BBC Scotland prepared a TV series, "The Secret Society," reporter Duncan Campbell uncovered a new satellite defence system unknown to MPs and the public. After MI5 raided the BBC and Campbell's home in a bid to stop the programmes, I decided to bring the Zircon affair into the public arena. Here I explain why.

When this newspaper first revealed the banning of the BBC's Zircon film, we little thought it would provoke such a fit of national hysteria. If, as we are now being told, the affair has reached the giddy heights of a political scandal, what exactly is the scandal about?

There were three strands to the story in our minds as we published it. There was the question of censorship. There was the banned revelation itself — that Britain was building a spy satellite to eavesdrop on the Russians. There was the claim that the £500 million cost had been illegally kept from Parliament.

It was hard to form an instant view on these matters. The country might need such a satellite, after all, and it might well need to keep its existence secret. How could one tell? Perhaps we could afford the additional defence burden; perhaps not. The BBC may have been acting responsibly and on the best advice in first commissioning and then stopping the programme. Or not, as the case may be.

These were not matters for us to decide. As journalists, our job was to present the facts to the public as we knew them, taking care not to stumble around clumsily in areas of ultra-sensitivity. We were urged at first not to identify the project as an intelligence satellite, for example, and we didn't.

Since then the so-called scandal has taken on many new forms, according to one's political perspective and capacity for outrage:

The Speaker's initial ban on MPs seeing the film in the House of Commons;

The distribution of bootleg videos around the country;

The Special Branch raid on the *New Statesman*'s offices;

The raid on the reporter Duncan Campbell's house;

The raids on the BBC offices in Glasgow;

The roles of the Attorney-General and the Scottish Lord Advocate in authorising these raids;

The Government's failure to act much earlier, before the film was even made;

The BBC's decision-making procedures;

And — always at the root of it all — the Official Secrets Act.

Howard Simons, managing editor of the *Washington Post* at the time of the Watergate affair, on a visit to London, was astonished and appalled by the attacks on the British media, and even more by the muted public reaction, 'If the police had gone in to the *Post*,' he told me, 'they'd have found Kay Graham lying in the doorway to stop them.'

Meanwhile, where were our society's self-proclaimed defenders of Truth, Freedom and Democracy? Not lying across doorways to protect the media, that's for sure.

In a piece that was wild even by his own trigger-happy standards, Paul Johnson went so far as to link the BBC's use of investigative reporters –

"a low form of journalistic life" — with share ramps in the City. He described the Secret Society series as "possibly the most damaging breach of national security for many years," ignoring the fact that the satellite project had been revealed last year in press hand-outs by British Aerospace.

Another rabid Left-to-Right convert, Lord Chalfont, branded the "muck-raking journalist" as a "traitor — ill-intentioned and irresponsible people making their own decisions about what is secret and what is not." He also claimed, however, that "Campbell's story was of very little real importance" — which made one wonder what he was getting so excited about. "Keeping Britain's secrets at all costs" was the *Daily Express* headline. At all costs?

If a government's job is to keep secrets, part of a reporter's job is finding them out. An editor's job is deciding whether to publish them or not. In doing this he may take advice and withhold a story in the name of national security (by using the D-notice system, for example, which seems to have been curiously inoperative over the Zircon affair). Or he may go ahead and publish anyway, on the grounds that the public ought to know. He may turn out to be right or wrong either way.

But what makes a journalist think he's entitled to decide about a state secret when nobody elected him to do that? The best answer I know to that common charge is contained in the remarks of an American judge in the Pentagon Papers case: "Security also lies in the value of our free institutions. A cantankerous press, an obstinate press, a ubiquitous press must be suffered by those in authority in order to preserve the even greater values of freedom of expression and the right of the people to know."

Governments, especially this one, fail to recognise that expressing a view about the national interest in a peacetime democracy is a matter for anyone. National security in time of war involves different considerations and may require some curtailment of this liberty by mutual consent.

Secrecy is not a simple concept. It is not just a reserved, adult body of knowledge to be kept from children. It goes very deep in human nature, for secrecy is at the core of power. To be a keeper of secrets confers status and identity. It was part of the divine right of kings. In this primitive system of values, power must be impenetrable. To let the public know is seen as a mark of weakness, a sharing or dissipation of power.

In Britain there is still a presupposition in favour of secrecy where, in a fully democratic society, there should be a presupposition in favour of openness. It took the public grilling of Sir Robert Armstrong by Malcolm Turnbull in Australia over the Spycatcher affair to bring this important truth painfully home.

Journalists live with secrets all the time. In a society like ours, where far too much information is classified (as the Franks Committee reported 15 years ago) you can hardly investigate anything at all without bumping into something supposed to be a secret. Even the Government's own lobby briefings to the Press are a secret and officially never take place.

This is a useful reminder that journalists don't invent secrets: secrets are given to them. Many of these leaks are deliberate, which journalists need to be wary about. As for giving things away to the enemy, there is nothing to compare with the record of the security services themselves, both here and in the United States. Traitors and defectors have left a far more deadly trail of havoc than a hundred Duncan Campbells could ever do.

This is why the security services have to be watched, too, and why journalists take an interest when they learn of defence programmes that by-pass Parliament and, in the case of Spycatcher, of our intelligence agents playing dirty tricks on allied countries and plotting against the elected Prime Minister.

A week that exposed the thin skin protecting our much-vaunted freedoms ended with two ironies. A Bill of Rights was voted out by MPs — and the Foreign Office had the nerve to invite 35 countries to London for an international conference on freedom of information.

Two, at least, of these countries would be impressed by our record in the Zircon affair: the Americans with Duncan Campbell and the Russians with our Special Branch.

The *Observer*, 1987

Malvolio plays Northcliffe

The launch of the *Independent* in 1986 was a glad bright morning for anyone who cared about the quality and integrity of the British press. The paper's subsequent upheavals are bound to excite equivalent concern.

Of the trio who founded it, Stephen Glover was the one with the lugubrious face, which makes his sprightly memoir all the more surprising. Even though (or maybe because) it burns with revenge, it is joyously entertaining.

The book (*Paper Dreams*, Jonathan Cape) falls into two distinct halves: a racy, anecdotal account of the launch of the daily, in which Glover appears as little more than a wry spectator, observing the success of the project with mounting amazement, and the story of his own rise and fall as founder-editor of the *Independent on Sunday*, which he naturally views in a more bitter and less detached way.

As he describes the early days of the *Independent* ("a kind of yuppy *Daily Telegraph*") he comes close to creating in Andreas Whittam Smith a rich comic figure of our time, given to a "red mist'" of rage at the slightest indignity, his face turning from chalky white to magenta, and a compulsive eater —with faint echoes of Malvolio, cross-gartered and all, in his "almost mystical belief" in his own genius as he calmly likens himself to Northcliffe (who, Glover points out, went mad).

As his own position is threatened, however, by a series of acutely felt betrayals, Glover's sense of humour begins to desert him. The portraits of Whittam Smith and Matthew Symonds ('Matty-puffs' to his Oxford girlfriend, Benazir Bhutto) become more demonic. A row between Matthew and Andreas over £10 is seen as the moment when "a grain of corruption entered into the soul of the *Independent*." The chief executive's "black Mercedes, with black leather seats and a blind in the rear window, looked like the car of a sinister African dictator." Even more portentously, "Tolstoy himself could not have guessed that beneath Matthew's bravado hid a stricken soul."

What remains astonishing about the *Independent*'s initial success was the lack of credentials of the group who started it. As Glover says, "We had an editor who had spent his life in financial journalism and a deputy editor and foreign editor who had never edited." In fact, they had a foreign editor (Glover) who had not even visited the United States and a features editor who had never worked on a newspaper.

Yet they raised the money, just, in what Glover cheerfully admits was a "glorious bluff": "The circulation projections were to prove optimistic and the profit ones wildly so; no dividend payments have been made to date." That bluff, it seems, may be about to be called.

They were lucky in their timing. They rode in on the high tide of entrepreneurial Thatcherism, with banks only too eager to help. It was a City Editor's dream. Having spent his life watching tycoons no cleverer than himself making fortunes, Whittam Smith's hour had come.

Conditions were right in Fleet Street too. Murdoch had just

achieved his Wapping revolution, releasing a refugee army of disgruntled journalists; the *Telegraph* was in a state of slow disintegration before its acquisition by Conrad Black; the *Guardian* had yet to start up its own presses. Newspaper barons were seen as the root of all evil.

On top of that, the Social Democratic Party was riding high in the opinion polls, so that the mould — in newspapers as in politics — seemed about to be broken. The new paper caught the public mood exactly. Its look and its tone had just the right flavour. It soon became, in Glover's words, "a fashion accessory."

The trouble with being fashionable, however, is that fashions change. The *Times*, *Telegraph* and *Guardian* soon got their acts together in the new non-union climate, and the recession starved the fledgling paper of advertising.

Whittam Smith's style of editing, distracted by his dual role as a wheeler-dealer, is described by his ex-colleague as "remarkably disengaged," like a king of medieval France, where the dukes and counts actually ran the place. Glover writes: "There was a vacuum at the centre of the paper where Andreas should have been" and "Andreas had an amazingly high tolerance of earnest journalism."

That earnest high-mindedness, which sometimes came over as sancti-moniousness, may have something to do with the fact that two of the paper's three founders were sons of the clergy (and the third, so it is rumoured, Asquith's unofficial grandson).

Glover's thesis — shared at the time by Lord Sieff, then the paper's chairman, and by one of its investors, Standard Life — is that the launch of the Sunday was a bridge too far and too soon, pushed through by Whittam Smith's unsinkable vanity against all economic logic. Glover's position on this, though accurate in retrospect, appears to lack moral and intellectual coherence, since he showed no reluctance to fill the new editorial chair.

He compounded his problems by having the Prime Minister, John Major, in to lunch at the office without inviting his editor-in-chief and allowing wayward spirits like Henry Porter and Stephen Fay to try to sell the paper off while Whittam Smith was in South America. That was asking for trouble.

Integrating the staffs of the two papers was not a resignation issue. It was to save costs, which Glover knew was necessary. Editors should not resign for reasons of pride; only principle.

The Sunday, launched in the depths of recession, forced the group through various stages of refinancing which seem likely to end either in the paper's closure or in Whittam Smith dividing his job or losing control of his empire.

Like the SDP, the *Independent* lost its momentum and its founders fell out. It languishes in bottom place in both its daily and Sunday markets — about 100,000 copies, so Glover reveals, behind the latest forecasts it gave its investors.

Glover concludes that it is "a great ship becalmed on a windless ocean"' That was before the *Observer*'s sale to the *Guardian* and the resignation of the new chairman, Sir Ralf Dahrendorf — both serious reverses for Whittam Smith — and the seizure of the Maxwell stake, against his wishes, by the people he calls "the southern Europeans", the Italians and Spaniards who may be poised to take control, putting at risk the paper's whole raison d'etre.

Suddenly, the ship is looking not so much becalmed as mutinous and starting to list in the water.

The *Observer*, 1993

CAMPAIGNING FOR DAVID GOWER

As an afterthought, we added a paragraph to our front-page story about the public outcry over David Gower's omission from England's winter touring party to India: "Readers wishing to support his reinstatement can write to us and we will forward the letters to the Test and County Cricket Board".

We received over 2,000 replies, from which we quoted extracts the following week. Our monster package of sorrow and anger was then passed on to the England selectors. One reader, Dennis Oliver, a Surrey businessman, launched a petition seeking a special meeting of MCC members to put a vote of no confidence in the selectors. I have joined the campaign and have been drumming up support.

The protest reaches its climax at Lord's, where the MCC President, Dennis Silk, the former Warden of Radley, and the Secretary, Colonel John Stephenson — flanked, it is rumoured, by the full weight of the Army and the Law in the form of Field Marshal Lord Bramall and Lord Griffiths, an eminent law lord (both former club Presidents) — will seek to persuade the 200-plus petitioners to drop their call for a special meeting. Against them will be ranged speakers as diverse as Lord Gilmour, the former Tory Cabinet member, and playwright Harold Pinter.

Pinter's presence will be a surprise, because he and I fell out badly during the Gulf War, when I refused to publish an obscene poem he had written about President Bush. When I taxed him about this, he replied: "Some things are more important than others, and cricket is one of them," In an earlier interview with the *Observer*, Pinter had famously said: "Cricket is better than sex."

Sex and poetry will no doubt be avoided by the MCC in the coming meeting in the Long Room. Instead, they will talk about money, arguing that the cost of a special meeting (put surprisingly high at £17,000) would be better spent on youth coaching than on debating a resolution which can have no effect, since the MCC cannot — indeed should not — seek to second-guess the selectors.

These views have been put to me vigorously over recent weeks by more than one senior club official ("Surprised at you, Donald, a former MCC Committee member too!). Even my colleague Alan Watkins has his doubts: "Seen Gower get out too easily too many times to treat him like a national monument". I'll try to explain to both sets of critics why the Gower campaign is a cause worth fighting for.

It would all have been avoided, in my view, if the Test and County Cricket Board had been quicker to respond to the public mood and the rational points raised by numerous cricket writers. They could have increased the size of the 16-member party on the grounds that the tour is an unusual one in having seven one-day internationals as well as three full Tests. Two of the party, Neil Fairbrother and Dermot Reeve, are one-day specialists, leaving only 14 for the Test matches. And sickness in India is hardly unknown.

Gower's omission cannot be explained on cricketing grounds. He has scored more runs for England than any player in history. He saved England twice last summer, demonstrating a mature responsibility he is said to have lacked in the past. We play six batsmen these days; no one could seriously argue that Gower, at 35, isn't still in the best three or four.

Unlike several players chosen ahead of him, he turned down lucrative offers to go to apartheid South Africa because he prefers playing for England. The sense of injustice — felt throughout the cricketing public — goes even deeper.

It is widely believed that Gower was omitted because his cavalier style of play and personality, grace before strength, offended the dour fitness-and-conformity regime of the England management; indeed, his cherubic countenance and mild sardonic manner were interpreted as dumb insolence. The clash of styles has been aggravated by personality factors on both sides, with the strong whiff of a personal vendetta.

There has always been scope for both styles in cricket, for Compton as well as Hutton, Botham as well as Bedser, Dexter as well as Boycott, Gower as well as Gooch. Cricket is both a team game and an arena for talented individualists. Team factors — discipline, coaching, fitness — have been rightly developed with the one-day game. But a batsman taking strike in a five-day Test match in Melbourne, Jamaica or Calcutta has to summon up reserves of talent and temperament from within himself that no amount of team talks, net practice or early nights can guarantee. Gower's record, especially against India, speaks for itself.

Gower himself has written: "I feel that my own fall from favour had a lot to do with the fact that so much fun had evaporated from Test cricket that anyone who looked as though he enjoyed it, particularly when things were not going well, was regarded with suspicion."

The present selectors are heavily loaded against individualism in favour of a management style more commonly found in football — inexplicable in the case of Ted Dexter, chairman of the England Cricket Committee, who showed great panache in his playing days and more taste, as I recall, for late nights than for press-ups or jogging.

In making a public protest that is probably unique in the game's history, cricket fans are dissociating themselves from the hurt and injustice done to a man for whose graceful, carefree approach to cricket and to life they feel a deep affection and gratitude. It is a blow for what they believe are the true values and spirit of the game.

Our quarrel is not with MCC, who no longer represent power and money in world cricket. But some members still look to the club, with its great traditions, as a focus for the higher values and standards of the game — values they believe to have been dishonoured in this case.

The Gower affair raises isues of honour and decency. As our readers pointed out, the campaign "transcends the narrow boundaries of international sport and impinges upon matters of morality and justice". "It is not their team, it is England's team. It is not their sport, it is ours." "It has tapped an honest rage too deep for tears."

Romantic, yes. Over the top, perhaps. Doomed, probably. Irresponsible, certainly not. Instead of being exasperated by the campaign, cricket's administrators should be glad of this remarkable demonstration that the venerable game still has a powerful grasp on public emotions.

The *Observer*, 1992

Message for the media

Goebbels, Hitler's propaganda chief, had a house with a spectacular view across the Wannsee on the edge of Berlin. On this very site the Aspen Institute held an international seminar on freedom of the press — and more ominously, freedom *from* the press. The irony was noted.

It brought together lawyers, journalists, academics and officials from the United States, West Germany, Holland and Britain. Any attempt to summarise or synthesise the talk would also falsify. Here are some random quotations — anonymous ones from the seminar itself, others from the background papers. The chief, perhaps only connection, is that they all found their way into this reporter's notebook:

"I am unable to understand how a man of honour could take a newspaper in his hands without a shudder of disgust" (Baudelaire).

"The media consistently help promote patriotism, faith in government and confidence in a moral order."

"Journalism is at best a quick glance at history on the run."

"The press used to be seen as protectors of the public, brave little men in grubby raincoats. Now the press is seen as a powerful institution, insensitive to the claims of small people, creating false pictures of society."

"A cantankerous press, an obstinate press, a ubiquitous press must be suffered by those in authority in order to preserve the even greater values of freedom (Judge in the Pentagon Papers case)."

"I'm with you on the free press: it's newspapers I can't stand (Tom Stoppard)."

★★★

"Reporters should, of course, be guided not only by a sense of legality, but also by a sense of decency and ethics."

"It's a rough old world out there, with some nasty people doing nasty things. Reporters need to be cunning."

"Reporters should never lie in pursuit of a story."

"A good writer is always selling somebody out."

"No area of a public man's life should be out-of-bounds to press inquiry if it affects, or might affect, other people's lives."

"All journalistic codes are moonshine (H. L. Mencken)".

★★★

"Your job requires you to pry, and mine requires me to keep secret (Dean Acheson to James Reston)."

"I recognise the right of a government to retain secrets. I do not recognise their right to recover secrets once lost."

"We don't have many big secrets left in Britain, but those we have are protected with lunatic care."

"America may have suffered from an excess of exposure. But it has suffered more from excessive secrecy."

"Would the Pentagon Papers case have been won if a less influential paper had been involved?"

★★★

"In Germany young people simply do not believe the Press. They mistrust it as a rotten part of a rotten system."

"The media are forced to be either police spies or terrorists' friends. They must be neither."

"West German police must not be identified in pictures and are free to snatch film from photographers' cameras."

"The media, especially TV, are too often seen as suckers for propaganda that helps the enemies of the State."

"Judges are generally on the law-and-order side, like most people in Germany."

"There is no word in German for investigative reporting."

★★★

"The agenda-setting function of a national Press has become almost frighteningly important."

"During the Tet offensive in Vietnam, White House staff listened to and believed the television reports rather than their own secret dispatches."

"We don't exist to serve governments. We exist to serve our readers. Too often, in fact, we serve only ourselves."

"It is painful for a society to learn that all is not well within itself, that its rulers are fallible, money is wasted, and bad decisions are made. So it blames the press."

"The Ship of State is the only kind of ship that leaks from the top."

"It isn't the press's fault if the Ship of State is a Ship of Fools."

★★★

"There are no friendly journalists."

"About half of the stories in the *Wall Street Journal* are barely rewritten press releases from the firms the stories are about (*Columbia Review of Journalism*)."

"Editing is what editors are for (Chief Justice Burger)."

The *Observer*, 1981

7 | COMRADES

SPORTS WRITER OF THE AGE

When Hugh McIlvanney retired from the *Sunday Times* in 2016 after 23 years on the sports pages, following a previous 30-year stint at the *Observer*, the tributes were remarkable. No reader could have been left in any doubt that he was the finest sports writer of the age.

As if this isn't enough, however, there exists an even larger claim for his talents: "Hugh McIlvanney is very probably the best writer ever to apply words to newsprint." That supreme accolade is contained in *The Great Reporters*, a global study by David Randall of newspaper writing from William Howard Russell's dispatches in the Crimean war to the present day. Even Hugh might have been embarrassed by such extravagant praise.

It is arguable, however that no sports writer can ever produce a comparable level of work in the future. There is no shortage of talent or energy in every generation of sports journalists, but no one will ever have the access McIlvanney and his generation enjoyed to the world's leading sportsmen and women and to the people around them. The protection of agents, publicists and clubs is already making it impossible for sports writers to become friends, as he did, with legendary figures like Muhammed Ali, Pele and George Best.

He also acquired a profound knowledge of football through mixing with the greatest managers, Matt Busby, Jock Stein, Bill Shankly and Sir Alex Ferguson (though a common background in the west of Scotland will have helped there too). Except through press conferences, this route is also mainly blocked.

I knew Hugh, as a colleague and a friend, for over 50 years. He leaves a huge gap in my life and in the lives of the relatively few friends he trusted enough to open up to. It is very hard to accept that one may never again pick up the telephone and hear that deep, mellow voice with the precious gift of making you feel that you were the only person in the world he wanted to talk to. In case that might sound a bit sentimental, I should add that the resulting conversation would often take the form of an icy blast in the ear if you had said or written something that fell short of his exacting standards.

We knew we were accepted as his friends when he commanded us to attend the many special occasions he wanted to celebrate. In his later years these were usually lifetime achievement awards he received from the ruling bodies in many of the sports he wrote about, and also included his marriage at the age of 80 to his beloved Caroline, also a writer, his long-term partner.

Hugh had joined the *Observer* from the *Scotsman* in 1963; I joined in 1966, the week England won the World Cup. One of our first pub conversations was about an altercation he had had with the England manager, Alf Ramsey, who had objected to something he had written. Ramsey had sneered at him at a press conference: "How many caps have you got?" When Hugh had eloquently defended his view, Ramsey muttered: "Words, words, words." Hugh replied: "Alf, they're very handy if you want to say something."

His sharp wit was evident at another press conference after Joe Bugner had been badly beaten by Muhammed Ali. "I'll fight anyone," declared Bugner defiantly, "even Jesus Christ." "Ah, Joe," said Hugh, "you only said that because you know He has bad hands." Hugh once said Bugner had "the physique of a Greek statue but fewer moves."

These flashes of wit, though typical of his conversation, belie the agony that went into his writing. He researched every detail, never accepting information from any source unless he had double-checked it himself. The reason he was so good is that he worked harder at it than anyone else. Harassed sports editors said that extracting his article was like pulling teeth. Once, when begged to release an article he had been labouring over for many hours, he said: "I just hate letting it go if it's not as true as I can make it."

On one occasion a sports editor rang Hugh to find out how he was progressing. He replied gloomily: "I'm having trouble with the colon." When the desk man offered sympathy, asking if he was in pain, Hugh replied: "No, I mean I can't decide if I need a colon or a semi-colon in this sentence I'm struggling with."

There is a famous story about him hearing from fellow football reporters on a train that a shot Hugh had described as hitting the crossbar had actually been pushed onto the bar by the goalkeeper. Hugh, horrified, insisted on getting off the train at Crewe and ringing through a correction to the report he had sent earlier (this was long before the mobile era or even TV replays). As a result, the train went on without him and he spent the night on Crewe station.

He used to refer to the pain of composing his weekly article as "the tunnel," out of which he could only emerge after a marathon struggle through the dark. He would usually start writing around Friday lunch-time after talking to everyone he could find and reading everything about the subject he could lay his hands on. He wouldn't finish much before dawn on Saturday, if then. In his earlier days, BC — Before Caroline, that is — he would then set off on a bender and sometimes go missing.

Any honest account of Hugh McIlvanney's life in newspapers cannot ignore the roistering of his early (and sometimes not so early) days. Sometimes, after a marathon drinking session, he would rely on his fists, rather than his wit, to win an argument. For that reason Alan Watkins, who had seen him in action in ElVino's, always called him "McViolence" (though not to his face).

The late Willis Hall, the playwright, once had lunch with McIlvanney and Jon Holmes, the sports agent, at the Garrick Club, where Willis was staying, and sent Holmes the following note afterwards. It gives some idea of Hugh's lifestyle at the time:

"Hugh stayed on, under the stairs, for several hours more — and I last caught sight of him, in convivial company, on the landing around 8pm as I headed for dinner. As I was going down for breakfast next morning, I spotted, under the chair he'd been occupying, a half-smoked cigar, which must have slipped from his nerveless fingers, and a lighter, which must have slipped from his fading memory. The Garrick Club's loss was probably Gerry's Club gain." (Gerry's Club in Soho was one of Hugh's favourite late-night haunts).

One Saturday I remember saying to the sports editor at the *Observer*: "I haven't seen Hugh's piece yet." He pointed to his secretary, who was busy on the telephone: "She's checking out his safe houses", he said, meaning places where Hugh had previously been known to land up in the early hours.

Together with colleagues in the newsroom, I once helped to put together a quick paperback about the siege of the Iranian embassy in London, where hostages were rescued by a daring SAS raid. We wrote the book in a week and assembled in the office on a Sunday morning to complete the final chapter. As we opened a door we found Hugh fast asleep with his head on the boardroom table. He looked up, opened one eye and grumbled: "The doorman perhaps, even a security man, but not the f★★★★★★ Editor."

A tabloid journalist tells a story about fighting him in a pub and suddenly lowering his fists, mesmerised by the sheer beauty of the language Hugh was using to insult him.

He once asked me to meet his two brothers in the Mermaid Theatre, across the road from our newspaper office. I went after first edition to find myself facing three broad backs at the bar. When I said the word "McIlvanney," all three spun round like gun-fighters in a Western saloon.

I was struck by the subtle shades of difference in their faces. The hard, four-square features of the eldest brother, Neil, seemed to be cut from the coal mining stock from which the family derived in Kilmarnock.

William, the youngest, who became a successful novelist, was gentler and more willowy, with a Clark Gable moustache. Hugh was a mixture of the two — tough, but with eyes that displayed a wry humour and a piercing intelligence that never left unchallenged any careless opinion or the faintest trace of pretentiousness.

From 1969, when I became deputy editor, to 1993, when I left the *Observer* (followed soon after by Hugh) it was my job to keep McIlvanney on the paper. This wasn't easy, because it didn't pay good salaries and Hugh was in great demand from papers that could offer him much more. Sometimes, when he had received an outside offer, we would sort things out over a bibulous lunch at the Garrick Club. Quite recently, when I was staying there, an old waiter said to me: "I thought you'd like to know that the record you and Mr McIlvanney set for lunch at the club all those years ago, finishing at 7.25pm, has now been beaten."

More often, though, Hugh would put his head round my door around six o'clock and say: "Donald, could we have a wee word? "I would ring my then wife and say: "I'm going out with Hugh McIlvanney." She would say: "See you in the morning." Off we would go into the night, usually ending up in the early hours in some seedy Soho drinking club, where we would sometimes engage in a bout of friendly arm wrestling and a tearful Hugh would swear his undying love for the *Observer*. "I'll never leave it," he would say.

Unfortunately, however, he did leave it in 1972 when the *Daily Express* doubled his salary. I warned him that they were only seeking his adjectival brilliance and, after a honeymoon period, would start cutting back on his space. In less than a year he rang me to say I was right and could he come back? He had rung the *Express* sports desk to ask what length of article he should write and was told 800 words. "800 words!" he exclaimed: "Jesus Christ, my intro's longer than that!"

When I became Editor myself in 1975, I expected someone else to take over McIlvanney duties, but there were no volunteers, so we carried on as before. The bond I had with Hugh was strengthened on the occasions he strayed from the sports pages onto territory I controlled. He led the front page with vivid reports on the Hillsborough disaster and the slaughter of Israeli athletes at the Munich Olympics. He also wrote a compelling account of Mike Tyson's trial for rape.

On the eve of the 1968 Olympic Games, when troops in Mexico City killed over 200 protesters, mainly students, and injured more than 1000, Hugh was sharing a room with Christopher Brasher, the athletics correspondent, who was a gold medallist. Both men insisted on writing the news story and had a row about it. They sent me separate intros and asked me to choose between them. I managed to persuade them that the seriousness of the story required them to work together, which they reluctantly did. They produced a superb report that led the paper.

Once, while Hugh was abroad, I shuffled around some paragraphs in the article he had filed. This was a daring thing to do, for nobody messed with McIlvanney's prose. I was expecting a nuclear confrontation when he returned to the office, but he saw the point of my changes and after that I sensed that our relationship had improved, once he accepted that I shared his feeling for words.

While Hugh took the high road to London and lived there for the rest of his life, Willie stayed in Scotland. But they remained close and admired each other's work. My wife and I have a lasting memory of a dinner where the two brothers, sitting at opposite ends of the table, sang a plaintive Celtic ballad as a duet with no accompaniment. It was quite beautiful and the room stayed silent for some time afterwards. Hugh's rendering of "Me and Bobby McGee" lit up many another evening.

He was nearly always lively, even exuberant company, with a stock of funny stories from his past. The only exceptions were when he had discovered a grammatical or other mistake in his published story or that, say, the name of a referee had been misspelled; then a gloom would descend that alcohol only served to deepen. He once famously rang the office in the early hours to ask the night editor to change a phrase from "late spring" to "early summer." The night editor's response is not recorded.

Hugh had a profound knowledge of literature, especially Shakespeare, and was a regular theatre-goer into old age. His muscular writing style was emphatically his own, an extension of his speaking voice, though if pressed he might have acknowledged traces of A.J. Liebling, Norman Mailer and Arthur Miller.

Politically, he was firmly of the Left, a staunch republican and a supporter of Scottish independence. I never asked him about Brexit, for as a Leaver I feared I might be blown out of the room. Recently, when the name of Boris Johnson came up in conversation, his rage took some time to subside.

He was such a perfectionist that even preparing a short speech was a form of torture for him. I remember him speaking at a memorial service for Richard Baerlein, the *Observer's* racing correspondent. St Bride's Church in Fleet Street spilled over with owners, trainers and jockeys, who were busy whispering and passing around bits of paper. I discovered that they were laying bets on how long Hugh's speech would take — an impossible calculation, since he was still scribbling additions to his text as he went up to the lectern.

Over 60 years in the newspaper business I have come across most of Britain's finest journalists and worked with a fair number of them. McIlvanney was the most exceptional writer and the most irreplaceable. He could also be a kind and generous man, easy to forgive, at least for those who loved him, when the dark clouds came down.

I am proud to look back on the tiny part I may have played in his career — not in relation to the writing, for that was all down to his own blazing talent and the painful labour that brought it to birth. But perhaps for helping at times, just a bit, to keep that might motor churning.

After we both reached 80, Hugh and I had a macabre, light-hearted wager as to which of us would speak at the other's memorial service. There are some bets it is very sad to win.

The *Sunday Times*, 2019

THE PRODIGIOUS CLIVE JAMES

Although Clive James was sometimes described as "the wittiest man in England," he remained defiantly Australian through more than six decades of living in Britain. "Wit" (in the 18th century sense) was his stock-in-trade, but his was not the kind of wit designed to conceal intellectual depth: it paraded and exulted in itself.

His great gift was that he could use his often hilarious phrase-making skill (he hated his jokes being described as "one-liners") across a vast range of media and that it appealed equally to popular and highly cultured audiences.

He first became well-known as a television critic, virtually inventing that comic genre, at the *Observer* from 1972-82, but he was also a novelist, poet, essayist, book reviewer, song-writer, television interviewer and documentary film-maker.

His rate of productivity in all these fields was prodigious. He published over 40 books of fiction, essays, poetry and autobiography. In his later years he built one of the most comprehensive and ahead-of-its-time websites (www.clivejames.com) to showcase his life and work. Apart from containing an archive of his own voluminous works, the website uses film and audio to carry his online interviews with leading figures in the arts and literature.

He related his obsessive creative energy to the early trauma he suffered when his father, just released from a Japanese prisoner-of-war camp at the end of the Second World War, died in an air crash on his way home to Australia in 1945. He believed that was the defining event in his life. "That's when I found out the world was arbitrary. At the age of six."

He reflected on this experience in a poem describing a pilgrimage he made to his father's grave in Hong Kong: "Back at the gate, I turn to face the hill / Your headstone lost again among the rest. / I have no time to waste, much less to kill. / My life is yours, my curse to be so blessed." The effect, as someone said, was to make him "drive himself to the limit of what it is possible to achieve in one lifetime."

Clive Vivian Leopold James was born in Sydney in 1939, just after the outbreak of war. He attended Sydney Technical College and Sydney University. After a year on the *Sydney Morning Herald*, he sailed to England in 1961, part of a generation of talented Australians — Germaine Greer, Peter Porter, Robert Hughes, Barry Humphries and Michael Blakemore among them — who were to enrich English culture in their various ways.

After three years of what he described as "a bohemian existence" in London — another way of saying he was heavily addicted to alcohol and cigarettes (he later sacrificed both to his hyperactive creative life — "I haven't time for hangovers") — he went up to Pembroke College, Cambridge, at the age of 26. He became President of the Footlights and started writing for literary magazines.

Apart from the jokes that made him addictive on a Sunday, his strengths as a TV critic were his vast range of interests — "from ice-skating to Beethoven quartets", as he once put it — and the exactness of his descriptions of performers. Two examples: "Twin miracles of mascara, Barbara Cartland's eyes looked like the corpses of two small crows that had crashed into a chalk cliff"; and "Perry Como gave his usual impersonation of a man who has simultaneously been told to say 'Cheese' and shot in the back by a poisoned arrow."

Here are some more samples of the wit and wisdom of Clive James, applied to his contemporaries:

"*I was wrong to suppose that Peter Sellers thought the world revolved around him. He thought the cosmos did too, and history, and the fates. Like every egomaniac, he behaved as if everybody else spent their day being as interested in him as he was.*"

"Peter Cook wasn't just a genius, he had the genius's impatience with the whole idea of doing something again. He reinvented an art form, exhausted its possibilities, and just left it. He didn't lose his powers. He just lost interest in proving that he possessed them."

"I quite like talking myself, but when Peter Ustinov was in the room there wasn't much point, you just had to listen. He was unimaginably, overwhelmingly gifted. You had to imagine a cross between Dr Johnson, Isaiah Berlin, Peter Sellers, and don't forget Charlie Chaplin — because Peter was a great mime too. He was inexhaustible. It was like talking to Europe, talking to history."

"As far as talent goes, Marilyn Monroe was so minimally gifted as to be almost unemployable, and anyone who holds to the opinion that she was a great natural comedian identifies himself immediately as a dunce...She was good at being inarticulately abstracted for the same reason that midgets are short."

"Mrs Thatcher started quoting St Francis within minutes of becoming elected, and scarcely an hour had gone by before she was sounding like the Book of Revelations read out over a railway station public address system by a headmistress of a certain age wearing calico knickers."

"To me, Sydney Opera House looks like a portable typewriter full of oyster shells, and to the contention that it echoes the sails of yachts on the harbour, I can only point out that the yachts on the harbour don't waste any time echoing opera houses."

Being bald, tubby and lacking a dress sense, James's decision to go in front of the TV camera seemed like a surprising career move, but he swiftly became a popular success in series such as Cinema, The Late Clive James, Saturday Night Clive, Clive James on Television, and so on, introducing British viewers, among other things, to crazy Japanese game shows. He also made documentaries that achieved high ratings on subjects such as the Paris fashions, Las Vegas, Japan and Formula One, and interviewed stars like Katherine Hepburn, Jane Fonda and Mel Gibson. He pioneered TV travel "Postcards," reporting from a dozen of the world's great cities.

Through all his time in television, however, he took pains to maintain his intellectual credentials with reviews and essays in the literary weeklies: The *Listener, New Statesman, Times Literary Supplement, New York Review of Books*, etc. He also published collections of his TV criticism and literary essays and began a series of autobiographical volumes with *Unreliable Memoirs*, which became a bestseller and has been reprinted 62 times. Apart from the first one, *Brilliant Creatures*, his novels were not so popular.

He viewed himself as an outsider, awkward and misplaced, and once said he felt "equally homeless in Britain and Australia." He attributed his success on TV to the fact that he couldn't be pinned down to a place in the British class system — "I counted as coming from nowhere."

The good opinion of the London literary set was what he valued most. He demonstrated this in a series of satirical poems, *The Fate of Felicity Fark in the Land of the Media* and *Peregrine Pryke's Pilgrimage through the London Literary World,* followed by *Britannia Bright's Bewilderment in the Wilderness of Westminster.* They included thinly disguised characters such as Marvin Grabb, the TV presenter, the Irish poet Seamus Feamus and the novelist Mag Scrabble.

Interviewers — and indeed, many of his close friends — found it hard to discern whether the real Clive James was the self-deprecating figure he painted in his memoirs, hapless and gauche, or whether that was just a clever disguise for a man with a giant ego. One of his friends, the late Ian Hamilton, said James wanted to be "read and seen by everyone, all at once."

In his later years he went back to the stage, and on the road around Britain and Australia, as song-writer for Pete Atkin, a singer and composer with whom he had first collaborated at the Cambridge Footlights and the Edinburgh Fringe. They made six albums together in what has been described as "pop-folksy post-graduate rock'n' roll."

He once observed of himself: "That song I wrote in which the refrain goes, I'm a Crying Man that everyone calls the Laughing Boy — that's pretty well true." There is certainly a more sensitive and vulnerable note in his poems, especially those written in his later years. In Son of a Soldier he wrote: My tears came late. I was fifty-five years old / Before I began to cry authentically. He insisted: "The poetry, for me, is always the centre of the whole business." He wrote many of the poems while at airports on TV assignments, or in the air, using intricate rhyming and metrical systems.

He became an unlikely friend of Princess Diana, who had enjoyed his television shows, and became her lunch-time confidant. He wrote about her with insight and feeling on her death. Though admitting he was sorely smitten, he also saw that she could be "a fruitcake on the rampage."

He won a number of press awards for his journalism. In 1992 he was made a member of the Order of Australia, in 1999 an honorary Doctor of Letters of Sydney University and in 2003 he received Australia's premier award for poetry, the Philip Hodgins memorial medal. In 2006 he was made an honorary Doctor of Letters by the University of East Anglia and was elected an honorary Fellow of the Australian Academy of the

Humanities. In 2008 he was awarded the George Orwell Prize for a lifetime's achievement in journalism and broadcasting. In 2012 he was awarded a CBE.

He was married to Prue Shaw, a scholar in Italian, who stayed in Cambridge while he spent the week in London in a converted warehouse full of books. Their marriage survived a late estrangement when an Australian model revealed that she and James had had an eight-year affair. One of his last books, an English verse translation of Dante's *The Divine Comedy,* was seen as being, in part, a conciliatory gesture to his wife.

He was first diagnosed with leukaemia in 2010 and in 2012 he said he was "close to the end." For the next seven years, however, despite being hospitalised for much of the time, he continued to pour out books of poems and literary criticism. He leaves a widow and two daughters.

The *Independent,* 2019

A MODEL FOR JOURNALISTS

There is a risk that Patrick O'Donovan's name will soon mean very little to young journalists, even though he died only four years ago at the age of 63. This is partly because his career as a front-line reporter was abruptly halted in the 1960s by the illness that was to dog him for the rest of his life. It is also because his reputation was overshadowed — in my view unfairly — by the more assertive person-alities of people like Malcolm Muggeridge and James Cameron.

I say "unfairly" because Cameron and Muggeridge, for all their many talents and virtues, owed their popularity as much, if not more, to their work as television performers than as newspapermen. On newsprint alone, Patrick surpassed them both.

There are other reasons why his reputation should suffer, especially with young people, by the contrast with Cameron and Muggeridge. Unlike them, he was not fashionably dismissive of those set above us. He had no illusions; but he made allowances. He didn't score points. A cradle Catholic, he saw people in power as equally entrapped in life's tangled web of sin and self-deceit.

In a rare outburst, provoked by the sight of Winston's Churchill's funeral, he wrote: "Britain just now is a curious country. It is the only country where patriotism is dismissed as a joke in bad taste and where treason, or what once passed for treason, is the fashionable manner of writing and talking... It is the one country where intellectually to destroy and to reject has taken the place of longing to build and create. And we give a lead in this respect which no other country in the world seems anxious or interested to follow."

He also lacked the peacock quality, the air of schoolboy show-off (at least in his writing) that seems to be necessary for a serious journalist to create a personal following in Britain — a quality shared in varying degrees by people like Kenneth Tynan, Bernard Levin, Peregrine Worsthorne and Clive James, to name but a few. Patrick's work was unmistakable, unlike anyone else's, but his own personality was rarely up-front (a phrase he would never have used).

Although he liked to claim that he was "an Irish peasant," his grandfather having come to England from a village near Clonakilty in county Cork, Patrick himself was unmistakably middle-class — son of a Harley Street doctor and sometime Conservative MP, educated at Ampleforth and Christ Church, Oxford, a major and tank commander in the Irish Guards in World War II.

His Oxford friends included "Nico" Henderson, later Sir Nicholas and British ambassador in Washington, and Robert Kee, the TV journalist. Michael Foot spoke at his funeral. When David Astor offered him a job on the *Observer*, on the basis of an essay he had written about one of the Bronte sisters, Patrick's mother wept: "You cannot be a seedy journalist."

It is no accident that he received greater recognition in the United States, where reporters tend to be better appreciated. He was honoured twice for his coverage of the old Eisenhower and young Kennedy courts (JFK insisted on calling him "Pat," which he hated). I re-read his description of the city of Washington while on a recent visit there and was struck by the exactness of his observation.

He also achieved a legendary status among Americans by once appearing drunk on a late-night television show. When, eventually, he was whisked off during a commercial break, a columnist observed: "O'Donovan slid off the screen and straight into the hearts of the American people." This short, carefully edited collection of his writing (*A Journalists' Odyssey,* Esmonde Publishing) — mostly from the *Observer*, plus a few late essays from the *Catholic Herald* — ought to carry him straight into the hearts of the British people.

In particular, it should be read by all journalists, actual or aspirant, if only to remind them that — for all the other razzmatazz the business requires — putting words on the page, the right words in the right order, is the only real secret of any newspaper's success. My one criticism of the book is that it is presented more as an act of piety than an act of celebration.

O'Donovan was never afraid of saying things simply and broke all the conventions of style. His prose owed something to the rhythms he had heard in church. His sentences hardly ever contained more than 20 words and often fewer than 10. They were invariably active rather than passive and never elliptical or allusive. His meaning was always unmistakably clear. It was a person-to-person communication, never a dry-as-dust dispatch. Every line exuded warmth, compassion, generosity. David Astor rightly compared him to John Betjeman.

He made his name in Africa, virtually rediscovering the Dark Continent in the late 1940s. His description of a black township in South Africa, reprinted after 35 years, begins: 'It is as if a ragged and despairing army had laid siege to the city...This army of rootless men has no part in the wealth or pride of South Africa. If such an army were parked outside my city, I should fear for the future of my people.'

He covered eight wars. He was the first to understand the cataclysmic nature of Mao Tse-tung's revolution in China, while others treated it as just another shambles. In 1949 he led the front page with this sentence: "Without a motion of defiance, or tragedy, Nanking has been abandoned like an old tent" (a sentence that prompted Michael Davie to apply for a job on the *Observer*). I remember another Patrick intro from the Korean War at a time when all public services had broken down in Seoul: "Today I shaved in white wine."

Some foreign correspondents burn themselves out, or grow bored, and find it hard to adjust to more sedentary pursuits. Not Patrick. After his fighting days were done, he developed a talent for set-piece reporting of great events that launched him on a second career. His description of Churchill's funeral is a classic of eyewitness reporting that still stands up 20 years after the television pictures have faded. To borrow a line from the piece: "It was beautiful in the way that great works of art are beautiful." He gave dignity and nobility to the whole profession of journalism — we all felt that if a man of such towering talent could apply his gifts to our trade then there must be something to be said for it.

Richard West, who had accompanied O'Donovan on some foreign assignments, said of him: "Patrick O'Donovan was one of the greatest literary correspondents, who not only wrote to please lovers of good English, but brought to the task a store of historical and cultural knowledge. He did not try to conceal his own reactions and feelings. He did not aspire to a spurious objectivity." Later *Observer* correspondents such as Neal Ascherson, Mark Frankland, Gavin Young and Colin Smith could be said to have followed O'Donovan's example.

Patrick was a scholar and used his later years to discover architecture, archaeology and history, all of which he conveyed in vivid terms to the reader. He wrote out of a profound sense of life's richness and complexity. He was reluctant to pontificate or to offer opinions, even in areas where he was undeniably expert. He never volunteered an idea for an article, yet he never turned other people's down. Somehow he managed to transmute anything into journalism — even the snails in his Hampshire garden and the nurses who lightened his last painful years.

The *Listener*, 1985

WATKINS, SUPREME STYLIST

Alan Watkins was one of the last of the great Fleet Street characters. He called his autobiography *A Short Walk Down Fleet Street* — a title that so confused an Islington bookshop that I was directed to the section on London streets. In fact, his was quite a long walk up and down Fleet Street, having started his career more than half a century before, in the era of Lord Beaverbrook — for whose retired mistresses he was required to wrap up gifts in brown paper parcels as part of his duties as New York correspondent of the *Sunday Express* — and ending it in the world of Google and Twitter.

Not that he allowed the digital world to intrude upon his well-ordered life. Until very recently he wrote his columns in long-hand, in ink on A4 paper, and dictated them by telephone to the *Independent on Sunday*. A creature of habit, he would then take a bus from his Islington home (it used to be a taxi until the paper economised on expenses) down Farringdon Road, where he would stop to buy a sandwich and a glass or two of champagne at El Vino's before catching the Docklands Light Railway to the office in Canary Wharf.

Looking dishevelled and faintly baffled, he would stare at a screen to ensure that no fool of a sub-editor had interfered with his subjunctives or his past participles. *Fowler's English Usage*, *Vacher's*, *Wisden* and *Bagehot* were his constant companions. An ex-student of W. A. Robson at the London School of Economics, he would have relished the constitutional niceties of a hung Parliament.

Watkins once wrote: "My entire working life has been spent in the quadrilateral enclosed by the Euston Road to the north, the Thames to the south, Goswell Road to the east, and Whitehall and the Charing Cross Road to the west. It includes Lincoln's Inn, the LSE, the *Sunday Express,* the *Spectator*, the *New Statesman,* the *Observer,* the House of Commons, El Vino's and the Garrick Club. This may be limiting but there it is and there we are and it cannot be helped."

He was my first new appointment as Editor of the *Observer* in 1975. I had tried earlier, while deputy to David Astor, to persuade Watkins to go to Washington for the paper. Although he turned the offer down, our friendship began then. I had admired his writing ever since I was an undergraduate at Cambridge. I always remembered his comment in the *Sunday Express* on Hugh Gaitskell's famous "fight, fight and fight again" speech at the 1960 Labour Party conference: "The speech was crude, vulgar, abusive and intellectually negligible. Inevitably, it was a great success."

When I interviewed Watkins for the job of political columnist in the Blackfriars pub, round the corner from the *Observer* — or rather, made my pitch, since he was much in demand — we became uncomfortably aware that we were being watched, and that we may even have been followed down the street. The man on surveillance duties, who appeared to be eavesdropping on our conversation from behind a pillar and scribbling in a notebook, turned out to be Geoffrey Wheatcroft. He was acting on behalf of the *Spectator*, which was also trying to poach Watkins from the *New Statesman*.

One reason the *Observer* won this recruitment beauty contest was that in the 1950s it had published the stylish political articles of Hugh Massingham, whom Watkins regarded as "one of the finest political writers of the post-war period" and on whom he would model his own columns.

Alan and I got on together because his greatest interests in life, outside politics and his family, were rugby, cricket, wine and the English language — interests which happened to coincide with mine. He had an exaggerated opinion of my judgement and competence and once said I would have made a good Chancery judge, which I took to be a compliment, since he was a qualified barrister. When he published *A Short Walk Down Fleet Street*, in which he described me, implausibly, as "the Rocky Marciano of newspaper politics," he told me that Anthony Howard, who was his brother-in-law, had upbraided him for being too nice to me.

About a year ago before he died, I was in the dining room at the

Garrick Club when he came in, spotted me, called my name and hobbled over on his walking stick. The room fell silent as I stood up. He whispered something in my ear, then hobbled off again. "What was that all about?" asked my companion. What Watkins actually said was: "Worsley for number seven with the Lions."

In El Vino's or the Garrick, when approached by someone whose company we didn't fancy, we would go into a comic routine in which we recited the names of great prop forwards of the 1950s. This was usually enough to drive away the most persistent of bores — in which category Watkins would sometimes include Howard, when Alan was in the mood for sport rather than politics.

He had more elevated table-talk, however, with the likes of Conor Cruise O'Brien, Frank Johnson, Philip Hope-Wallace, Peregrine Worsthorne, Terry Kilmartin or the snooper Wheatcroft.

Watkins features in my favourite expenses story. One day my managing editor at the *Observer* showed me a letter he was sending to Alan, saying: "You have claimed for a lunch bill on expenses, yet only one person seems to have eaten. As you know, the company does not pay for members of staff eating on their own." The next day he showed me Alan's response, scrawled at the top of the letter: "He ate. I drank."

His *Private Eye* sobriquet, Alan Watneys, belies the sophistication of his drinking. He may have drunk beer with MPs in Annie's Bar in the House of Commons, where he made some of his earliest and best political contacts, but in my company he preferred wine or champagne (maybe because I was usually paying).

I never saw him drunk or the slightest bit aggressive. In fact, the more he drank the more he seemed to retreat within himself and enjoy watching others making fools of themselves. Watkins had that most precious gift in a journalist of perfect verbal recall, especially when a politician was gabbing on unguardedly. He made a study of politicians' favourite tipple and I remember his shudder of distaste on discovering that Nigel Lawson drank Spritzer.

An equally valuable gift, like that of a theatre critic, was his ability to write seriously about politicians in a style that was easy to understand and also very funny. Here are some of my favourites:-

"Mr Blair reminds me of the newly arrived Welsh preacher whose qualities were being assessed by two women chapel-goers: 'He is a fine-looking man, no mistake about that.' 'With a melodious voice.' 'And so powerful in prayer.' 'What a pity he's such a bloody liar.'"

Of David Cameron he used to say: "Once a PR man, always a PR man."

Talking to Sir Edward du Cann, he said, was "like descending a staircase in the dark and missing the final step. You are not hurt but you are mildly disconcerted."

His final published words were about the pre-election debates in 2010: "Mr Clegg is adept at the soft answer that turneth away wrath. He does not have anything to teach Mr Cameron; still less poor Mr Brown, who chews gum even when he does not have anything to chew…Mr Clegg turned Mr Brown's blandishments aside, as if he were a beautiful girl who was rejecting the overtures of an ageing roué."

I rarely interfered with Alan's copy and sometimes had to head off John Cole, my deputy, when he wanted to challenge some comment Alan had made, usually about trade unions or Ireland. The few interventions I made were when I thought he assumed too much knowledge of readers. Once I took him aside and said: "Alan, you and I remember that Ted Short was deputy leader of the Labour Party, but there aren't many of us left." He solemnly agreed and thenceforth poor Ted Short was consigned to the dustbin of history.

Alan did not seek newspaper scoops, but he received a great one for the *Observer* when Michael Foot (whom he always described as "the old bibliophile") rang him (and no other journalist) to say that he was standing for the leadership of the Labour Party.

Watkins left the *Observer* soon after the *Guardian* takeover in 1993. When *Guardian* executives made their first address to the *Observer's* staff, he was heard to mutter: "They're a conquering army. I'm off."

He once told me (perhaps influenced by working under John Junor) that he only ever had truck with editors: "I don't take any nonsense from underlings because the editor is the only one who can fire you."

He said he regarded himself as a man pushing a barrow along Fleet Street with something to sell. He would stop off at one paper as long as they wanted his wares. When he or they had had enough, he would up his barrow and move along the street. Even at the age of 77, he never ran out of clients.

The *Independent*, 2010

THE IMPOSSIBLE NORA

Nora Beloff was the first female political correspondent of a major British newspaper, a pioneering distinction that meant little to her. She took greater pride in the fact that she was uniquely qualified for the job, having spent the two previous decades as the *Observer's* correspondent in Paris, Washington and Moscow.

She was a tiny woman of terrier-like tenacity who always seemed to be in a hurry. Essentially a cold war liberal, she was a crusader by temperament and conviction, whether pursuing Trostskyists in the Labour Party, exposing the plight of Soviet Jews, defending the Serbs or fighting a trade union closed shop for journalists.

She was brave in pursuing causes that made her unpopular and sometimes exposed her to ridicule and physical danger. In her sixties she was arrested in the Soviet Union and expelled from Yugoslavia after being grilled by the secret police.

Her energy in pursuing divisions within the Labour Government led the then Prime Minister, Harold Wilson, to summon her editor, David Astor, to Downing Street in a forlorn attempt to get her sacked. He also hinted that he was having her followed to find out who her sources were. This story led the front page of the *News of the World*.

During her spell in Moscow she caused so much trouble to the Soviet authorities that when I went there many years later to ask for the *Observer's* accreditation to be restored, the Kremlin apparatchik muttered over and over to himself in remembered dismay, "Nora Beloff, Nora Beloff..." When I finally made him understand that she had left the paper soon after I became the Editor, I was treated like a hero of the Soviet Union and the red tape was magically cut.

Her international experience gave her a wider frame of political reference than her male colleagues at Westminster, an advantage she did not hide from them. Like many trail-blazing women, she attracted snide comments. In her case this led to a reputation, not wholly undeserved, for getting things wrong. This attitude was once expressed in her hearing in the Commons by Michael Foot, who drew loud laughter and applause when he said: "Honourable members may say that if Nora Beloff says it positively and with assurance, one could be quite sure the opposite is almost certain to be true".

A fellow lobby correspondent, Frank Johnson, came closer to the truth, however, when he wrote: "On large matters — as opposed to details of names, dates and the like — I would wager her record of accuracy to be as good as most of her competitors". Her main offence, he pointed out, was that she was a good deal cleverer than them. Her reporting on Trotskyist infiltration of the Labour Party in the late-1960s and early 1970s — later shown to have been substantially correct — angered some colleagues on the paper to the point where they complained to Astor through the National Union of Journalists.

As "Ballsoff", she became a favourite butt of *Private Eye,* which was fed snippets about her by jealous colleagues and rivals. She successfully sued them for libel when Auberon Waugh jestingly implied that she had slept with the entire Conservative Cabinet. But she lost a more celebrated case against the magazine when she was unwisely advised to sue them for breach of copyright when they published an office memorandum by her containing off-the-record information from a Cabinet Minister about Robert Maxwell. The case, which she lost on a technicality, set a damaging precedent for freedom of the press.

Nora could be a sore trial to the *Observer's* executives and sub-editors required to cross-check every fact in her copy. She had an annoying habit of getting her own way. Even when she seemed to have been comprehensively defeated in conference, she would sometimes persuade the editor, David Astor, to her point of view when he gave her a lift to work in his car from St John's Wood, where they both lived.

It was a weekly miracle that her column ever reached printed form, since she could barely type and took no serious interest in the craft of writing. She prevailed upon friendly colleagues to convert her frenzied scrawl into a publishable story. Sometimes, when they were not around, she could be heard in the newsroom, late on a Saturday afternoon, long after her deadline, desperately dictating her column to the copytakers from scraps of paper.

She came to an unusual arrangement with her opposite number at the *Sunday Times*, whereby they exchanged each other's stories in mid-afternoon, to ensure that neither would be taken by surprise. The arrangement came to light when she wandered nonchalantly over to the news desk and told them what the rival paper would be leading on. She was baffled by the managing editor's resulting apoplexy.

The fact that she had met most world leaders — Ho Chi Minh, the Vietnamese leader, gave her a red rose and petit fours and J.F. Kennedy offered her a lift in his car — and had been present at nearly every major event of the post-war era, gave her a self-confidence and lack of deference for British politicians unusual among lobby correspondents of the time.

One of the choicest amusements for colleagues was to overhear her, not so much interviewing as haranguing politicians on the telephone. "Come on, Reggie, don't be so pathetic", I once heard her to say to Reginald Maudling, then Deputy Prime Minister. "What you really think is this...and that's what I'm going to quote you as saying."

She once wrote of herself: "Journalism was obviously the right choice. I had the necessary qualifications: inexhaustible stamina, insatiable curiosity and a thick skin". She had all three to an advanced degree. She quoted with pride a comment by Richard Crossman that he knew nobody except Harold Wilson who bounced so quickly out of embarrassment.

She illustrated this quality over dinner at David Astor's house when she upbraided him over his treatment of a colleague. Filled with rage and alcohol, she paused in her torrent of words to vomit into her handbag, which she then snapped shut and carried on talking as if nothing had happened.

She was born in London into the intellectual Beloff clan on 24 January, 1919, the middle child of five. Max (Lord) Beloff was her elder brother. One of her sisters married a Nobel Prize–winning scientist. She was named after the emancipated heroine of Ibsen's *The Doll's House*. Her parents were Russian Jews. Nora herself was agnostic and renounced her mother's passionate Zionism. She went to King Alfred's School in Hampstead and read history on the eve of war at Lady Margaret Hall, Oxford, where Denis Brogan was one of her tutors.

She joined the political intelligence department of the Foreign Office and was sent to the Paris embassy. She stayed in Paris after the war and had spells with Reuters, the *Economist* and the *Manchester Guardian* before Brogan persuaded Astor to appoint her Paris correspondent of the *Observer* in 1947.

In the 1950s she moved to Washington and Moscow and held the political job from 1964-76. She was never happy with the paper after Astor's retirement, when I replaced her as political correspondent. She left in 1978 after a period as a roving reporter in Europe.

Her manner of leaving was typically chaotic. She wrote two letters — one a bland note to me, the other to the Americans who had bought the *Observer*, urging them to appoint another editor. Unfortunately for her, she put the letters in the wrong envelopes.

Neither retirement nor illness slowed her down. She remained as active as ever, travelling widely in the Communist countries and writing tirelessly to the papers on international issues. She wrote five books, of which the first, *The General Said No*, was a vivid insider's account of the abortive negotiations for British entry, and the last, *Tito's Flawed Legacy,* was translated into several languages.

Nora had a romantic side that few outside her family ever saw. Her newspaper colleagues were amazed, for example, to read this line in her book, *Transit of Britain*: "When I was seven I remember waking up one day to think this must be the happiest day of my life, as I was to play netball in the morning and be taken by mother to Golders Green Hippodrome in the afternoon to see Pavlova dance. I loved leaping around to the sound of music".

Her colleagues were even more amazed when, without warning at the age of 58, she suddenly married Clifford Makins, the *Observer's* gifted but somewhat shambolic sports editor.

For all her quirks and obsessions, Nora Beloff had one of the most distinguished careers any woman has had in British journalism, an achievement that deserved greater recognition than she received from her peers.

The *Guardian*, 1997

JANE BOWN'S GENTLE EYE

Jane Bown was an outstanding portrait photographer who confounded the experts with the simplicity of her camera technique. She spent 65 years on the *Observer*, for whom she took several thousand pictures of politicians, bishops, actors, pop stars and other celebrities, as well as ordinary people — miners, hop-pickers and women at a holiday camp — whose faces captured her interest.

Nearly all her pictures were snatched on location during the 10 or 15 minutes she was allowed while a reporter was interviewing someone for the newspaper. A tiny, round-faced, unobtrusive woman, she would appear with only a shopping bag, in which her camera would often compete for space with vegetables for that night's supper.

This unthreatening demeanour had the effect of defusing a subject's initial hostility. Both the Beatles and the Rolling Stones took to her and allowed her to stay long after the time allocated by their minders. This resulted in famous portraits of Mick Jagger and John Lennon in particular; she found Paul McCartney "a bit pompous."

Her much-admired picture of Samuel Beckett, showing his face as a cracked desert of lines protruding from a white polo-neck, was snatched at the stage door at the Royal Court after he had declined to see her. A very determined character beneath a gentle, nervous manner, she obtained a memorable portrait of Richard Nixon by crawling through the legs of the crowd outside his hotel and shouting to him to look at her.

She worked only in black and white. She was asked to try colour for the *Observer* when it launched a colour magazine in the 1960s, but she didn't like it and soon abandoned the experiment. She also used natural light; the only equipment she ever allowed herself was a table lamp, which she occasionally carried around to illuminate a face when the light was especially bad. She never used flash or an exposure meter.

At first she used a Rolleiflex, moving on to a Pentax and finally to her beloved Olympus camera with an 85mm lens, always at a camera speed of $1/60^{th}$ of a second and with the aperture at f2.8. The combination of wide aperture on a close-up lens produced a very thin depth of field. She focused on the subject's head, especially the eyes, and caught their faces in a way that isolated them sharply against a hazy background.

Lord Snowdon said she was "a kind of English Cartier-Bresson" who produced "photography at its best. She doesn't rely on tricks or gimmicks, just simple, honest recording, but with a shrewd and intellectual eye."

Jane Bown's origins were obscure. Her mother was a private nurse, working at Eastnor in Herefordshire, who fell inconveniently pregnant from a patient she was caring for. The date was 1925, but she was never sure of her birthday. Nor did she ever know the name of her father, but gathered that he was "posh...his family had land." She was farmed out to her mother's five sisters in Devon and Dorset (all named after plants: Primrose, Daisy, Violet, Iris and Ivy), who passed her around between them.

When she was 18, she joined the Wrens and worked as a chart-corrector for naval operations, including the D-Day landings. After the war she was given an education grant and chose to study photography at Guildford College, even though she had never held a camera before.

She took wedding photographs for a time until her former tutor, Ifor Thomas, having spotted her natural talent, put her in touch with Mechthild Nawiasky, the artist, who was working on the picture desk at the *Observer*. Nawiasky showed David Astor, the editor, Jane's college portfolio, and he was so impressed, especially by her picture of the eye of a cow, that he commissioned her to photograph Bertrand Russell, the first of her great *Observer* portraits.

In 1954 she married Martin Moss, a fighter pilot in the war who became a senior retail executive and is credited with turning Knightsbridge into a prime shopping location. They had a house in Alton,

Hampshire, and later moved to Alresford, into a Queen Anne house that had once been occupied by Jane Austen's brother.

Jane Bown spoke often about her subjects, in her usual staccato sentences, especially if they were boring (Robert Redford was one of those) but rarely about her art. She said once: "The best pictures are uninvited. They are suddenly there in front of you. But they are there one minute and gone the next."

Bjork said of her: "She can look at a person and she knows, instinctively, straightaway, who they are." Jane liked Gordon Brown and showed him laughing, but never caught Tony Blair. Asked about this, she said: "Oh, he was difficult. I just couldn't get him. I'm not sure there was anything there."

Once, in my early days on the *Observer*, I went with her to interview Sir Anthony Blunt, the art expert. The picture did not appear in the paper then, but it surfaced some years later when he was exposed as a Soviet spy. It showed him as sinister, half in light and half in shadow. Asked if she had sensed something sinister about him at the time, she said: "It wasn't me. It was the camera. It saw something creepy in his face."

Although she was clearly one of the great photographers of the age, she only became widely known to the general public after the *Guardian* Media group bought the *Observer* in 1993 and put her archive of pictures online and produced a documentary film about her. She had two exhibitions at the National Portrait Gallery and received an honorary doctorate from Southampton University. She published 11 collections of her photographs.

She was awarded an MBE in 1985, upgraded to CBE in 1995. When the Queen asked her what she did, she said was "a hack." Later, when she took the official photograph for the Queen's eightieth birthday, Jane herself was 81. She died eight years later.

The *Daily Telegraph*, 2014

ALAN ROSS, POET OF SPORT

Alan Ross was the most lyrical of sports writers in both prose and verse, as befits a poet who also kept the London Magazine afloat through five decades. He was football correspondent of the *Observer* from 1950-54 and cricket correspondent from 1954-72.

His best insights on cricket stand comparison with those of Neville Cardus and his own hero, R.C.Robertson-Glasgow, also an *Observer* writer (for whom he once batted against Oxford University). Cricket has occasioned some of the worst poems in our literature, but many of the good ones are his.

Hearing a long afternoon's conversation between Ross and E.W. Swanton, as I once did in the Committee Room at Lord's, gave a privileged glimpse into a lost world of cricket in which character, style and civilised values had more relevance than statistics.

Ross wrote at a golden time for English cricket and it seems incredible now that he covered six overseas tours and never saw England lose a series. They even won in Australia and the West Indies.

Born into a rich English family in India, he was sent to school at Haileybury, where he played in the last XI before the war. He went up to St John's College, Oxford, with Kingsley Amis and Philip Larkin. He played cricket for Oxford in the 1941 Varsity match before joining the navy, where he took part in violent action on destroyers.

His fractured background left him with a rootless quality that gave him a fresh and original eye as a writer, but may have contributed to bouts of depression that sometimes brought him close to the edge. He was nevertheless a lively companion with a bohemian taste for good wine and attractive women.

Apart from his lyricism, his greatest strength as a cricket correspondent, like Kenneth Tynan's as a theatre critic (both were writing for the *Observer* at the same time) was his ability to describe performers with an exactitude that pinned them to the page. On Len Hutton going in to bat against Ray Lindwall, for example: "Thus does a keeper, entering the cage, sense the tiger". He also wrote of Hutton: "Eloquent as sculpture in your driving, you fended down bouncers as you might unruly dogs".

He captured Ken Barrington's "curious leaning away stroke to the off — rather like waving away a footman and avoiding a fly at the same time". He described Ian Botham as "that wholly adventurous superstar, half charlatan, half avenging angel", deplored Geoffrey Boycott's "blinkered cussedness" and saw Curtly Ambrose "high-stepping like a show pony... mouth like a slice of cut papaya".

Ross the poet was at his best with players of natural grace like Colin Cowdrey, Tom Graveney and David Gower. Of Cowdrey he said: " He made the art of batsmanship an extension of his own geniality...At his best he was a dolphin among minnows...delicate in his responses to the invisible strings of memory and music...a false note and he is becalmed, devoid of will and wizardry". On Gower: "He and the bowler seem accomplices in an illusory magic".

He was at his happiest in the sea-scented air at Hove, watching Jim Parks at the wicket, then remembering Parks's father batting there two decades before and ruminating on the passage of time. Or watching his beloved Spurs at White Hart Lane. He wrote a poem linking Gary Lineker to the music of Satie and the paintings of Seurat.

One of his best poems is a hymn to Stanley Matthews — "horseless, though jockey-like and jaunty":-

> Expressionless enchanter, weaving as on strings
> Conceptual patterns to a private music, heard
> Only by him, to whose slowly emerging theme
> He rehearses steps, soloist in compulsions of a dream.

My favourite Ross poem is "Watching Benaud Bowl":-

> Leg-spinners pose problems much like love,
> Requiring commitment, the taking of a chance.
> Half-way deludes; the bold advance.
>
> Right back, there's time to watch
> Developments, though perhaps too late.
> It's not spectacular, but can conciliate.
> Instinctively romantics move towards,
> Preventing complexities by their embrace,
> Batsman and lover embarked as overlords.

In a book he inscribed to me, Ross wrote about sports writing:"There are no perfect similes, but one can try to preserve a style, restore an action, rehearse an elegance". Rehearsing an elegance was the story of his life.

The *Observer,* 2001

8 | FALLEN HEROES

CRICKET'S MASTER CRAFTSMAN

I got to know Sir Len Hutton when he wrote for the Observer *and we played golf together. I made a BBC TV programme about him in 1988, 50 years after his record innings of 364, and also edited a book about him. I wrote this tribute when he died.*

L en Hutton was one of the greatest and wisest of all cricketers, the first professional captain, and scorer of the highest Test innings (364) by an Englishman.

The Yorkshire club, unwontedly effusive, described him as "every boy's hero and the cricketer every man wanted to be".

Between 1934 and 1956, when he was knighted on his retirement, he scored 40,000 runs, including 129 centuries, at an average of 55. But, as R.C. Robertson-Glasgow warned, "to admire Len Hutton merely for the quantity of his runs is like praising Milton for the length of *Paradise Lost.*"

It was a Lancastrian, Neville Cardus, who captured the essence of the Hutton style: "A strength that is generated effortlessly from the physical dynamo, through nerve and muscle, so that we might almost persuade ourselves that the current of his energy, his life-force, is running electrically down the bat's handle into the blade." Edmund Blunden, the poet, saw something similar when Hutton broke Bradman's world record at the Oval in 1938: "His body and his bat were as truly one as love itself".

The son of a joiner, Len always relished the feel of a cricket bat. He kept this first one under his pillow to touch fondly in the night. Once he picked up Ian Botham's bat in the nets at Lord's: "It's like a railway sleeper," he said in wonder, having been obliged to use a light bat himself after a war-time injury. Even when he was over 70, at Alf Gover's cricket school, I watched him pick up some new bats and feel their texture lovingly, like a baby with a blanket.

Of his contemporaries, only Hammond and Compton were in the same class. From his teenage years with George Hirst and Bill Bowes at the Headingley "Shed", Hutton paid a craftsman's attention to batting technique. "He plays so close to the ball," said Cardus, "so much over it, that he has acquired a sort of student's slope of the shoulders; at the sight of a fizzing off-break he is arched like a cat". Technique, combined with an uncommonly quick eye and formidable concentration (his 364 took 13 hours 20 minutes, the longest innings in history), made him, along with Jack Hobbs, the most accomplished opening batsman of the century.

The style was the man. His success was as much a triumph of character as technique. In Barbados in 1986, when England were being destroyed by the West Indies fast bowlers, I said to Peter May, the frustrated chairman of selectors: "I doubt if anybody could play these people on this pitch." He looked up sharply and said: "Len could. He batted 10 hours on the 1954 tour and showed us all how to do it. We were two Tests down, but we drew the series after that. It just needs one man."

Len Hutton was that man too often. For much of his career he carried the England batting, a burden that took its toll on his nerves and physique and caused his early retirement.

The Bishop of Liverpool, David Sheppard, a former England batsman and long-time student of Len, told me that the clue to his elusive personality was to be found in the Protestant movements of Bohemia. The Huttons, in fact, were brought up in the Moravian community at Fulneck, near Pudsey, Leeds, founded by Count Zinzerndorf, who came here from Czechoslovakia in the 1730s.

It was an austere upbringing — "strict but caring", as he later described it. He had three devoted aunts who watched over him like guardian angels. His genius for cricket was spotted early by Herbert Sutcliffe, the great Yorkshire and England batsman, who played with Len's father and brothers at Pudsey St Lawrence, but he also developed a talent for soccer. One day, when he had injured his knee, he arrived home to find that his aunts, all silently knitting after a family conference, had put his football boots on the fire, a burnt sacrifice to his future destiny.

His shrewd sense of cricket's inner mysteries made him successful as a captain, winning and retaining the Ashes against Australia (though, strangely, he never captained Yorkshire), and later as a Test selector and writer on the game, enlightening *Observer* readers for close on 30 years. Though usually terse and taut as his batting, his writing was often enlivened — like his conversation in his more relaxed later years — by wry flashes of deadpan understatement which got funnier the more you thought about them, and which those around him learned to treasure and share with each other as "Len-isms".

Asked what he thought of a once fashionable England player, he replied carefully, wrinkling his famous "knob of garlic" nose (which contrary to legend, was not inflicted by a demon fast bowler, but from a misdirected throw by a wicket-keeper): "Well, he lacks something at the highest level, some quality...there's a word I'm seeking....it'll come to me in a minute...Then, with a twinkle and a flattening of vowels: "I've got it! Ability...that's the word I'm looking for."

On one occasion I met him at Lord's at an MCC dinner, just as he was being besieged by Essex supporters who were trying to make him say that their local hero was a great player and captain. One of them said: "But Sir Len, you must admit that he knows a great deal about the game." I knew Len had reservations about the player in question, so I wasn't surprised when he gave me a wink and replied cryptically: "The thing is, in this life, you can know a great deal about something and still be wrong."

His family were a source of great pride and pleasure to this very private man. He told me that he enjoyed watching his grandchildren play cricket more than Test matches, though he was a faithful attender to the end. He rang me the week before he died and arranged to come in for a cricket lunch at the *Observer*. I asked him about Gooch's 333 at Lord's. He said Gooch was always the most likely modern player to challenge his record.

He then praised young Tendulkar, who reminded him of another Indian, Gavaskar. "They both have little feet, you see," he added. I passed on this story to the chairman of Yorkshire cricket, Sir Lawrence Byford, who was delighted. "I want to bring in Tendulkar as the county's first non-white guest pro. If I can say that Len thinks Tendulkar will be a great player, that will help me beat off the opposition of the old die-hards on the committee." And so it proved.

Len had an obsession about the size of a batman's feet. Once, after watching Bradman hit England all over the field, he went to the Australian's dressing-room and discovered the secret of his genius: "I looked at his boots — they were the same size as Fred Astaire's!" He enjoyed expounding the theory — how seriously I could never tell — that the main reason why batsmen like Colin Cowdrey and Viv Richards were not as good as Bradman was that they had big flat feet, which meant that they couldn't drive as nimbly at the pitch of the ball and keep it down.

He also had a theory about hands, as I learned when I played golf with him. As I peppered wild shots all over Wimbledon, I suddenly heard this voice behind me: "It's all in the hands, Donald." He then demonstrated how great stroke-players like Cowdrey and Tom Graveney had a sure touch with the irons. Whenever I play golf now, I shall always hear that gentle Yorkshire voice of admonition: "It's all in the hands, Donald."

He was forced to think about hands after breaking his arm in the gym during Royal Marine training in the war. It was broken badly, in several places above the wrist, requiring a number of operations and skin grafts from his leg. When it was over, he found that his left arm, the guiding force for a right-handed batsman, was more than two inches shorter than the other. There was a serious chance, at the age of 25, that he might never play again.

As it was, he missed six years' cricket because of the war — at his prime from the age of 23-29 — and returned a different player. He had to change his technique, playing with a boy's bat and eschewing shots like the hook, which limited his repertoire against fast bowling. As E.W. Swanton said: "Given a full career without intermission or accident, who can tell what his record might have been?" Len was a man without bitterness, though I once heard him express a moment's sadness over what might have been.

We were lunching at the Garrick Club and an ageing member came over to say he'd never forgotten a brilliant innings Len had played in South Africa in 1939. "Ah yes," Len said, "1939 – everybody remembers 1938, but I was actually better in 1939. I was nearly as good as Bradman. After the war, of course, I was a different man. I'll never know how good I might have become in those lost years. I might not have got any better at all. The trouble is, you see, I'll never know."

People sometimes said that he was a hard Yorkshireman, selfish and ungiving. He was certainly hard in his playing days, as he had to be. Of the old enemy he once said: "In Australia the pitches are hard, the ball is hard, and the men are hard. You have to be harder to beat them." When it mattered he was, and he did.

But that is not how he should be remembered. He was unfailingly courteous and modest, with a hidden reserve of humour in those wide-apart blue eyes that never missed a trick, and he had a knack of making people feel they were his friends. I am haunted, as I know he was, by an Observer profile which had said he was "not lovable", if only because he didn't care whether he was loved or not. I think he did care, though he needn't have worried about it.

The *Observer,* 1990

GREATEST OF THE GREAT

He always said he was "the greatest" — and he was. But white America took some years to accept that the "uppity" black heavyweight from Louisville, Kentucky, who had refused to fight in Vietnam and changed his name to join the hated Black Muslims, was the greatest sportsman of the age and one of the world's most vivid and best-known personalities.

First as Cassius Clay and then as Muhammad Ali, he was idolised and vilified in almost equal measure until he achieved the status of a global icon, being named Sportsman of the 20th Century by *Sports*

Illustrated magazine and Sports Personality of the Century by the BBC. He is the only man to have won the world heavyweight championship three times. His presence, recognised all over the world, made people smile and he had that priceless gift of being liked as well as admired.

For the last three decades of his life, a form of Parkinson's disease stole from him both the strength and startling beauty of his prime, reducing a supreme athlete to a stumbling (though always dignified) shadow of his former self. This sad sight became a compelling argument for abolition of the sport to which he devoted his life.

He took part in some of the greatest fights in the history of boxing: three with his most formidable challenger, Joe Frazier, including the so-called 'Fight of the Century' in New York in 1971 (which he lost on points) and the 'Thriller in Manila' (which he won when Frazier couldn't rise from his stool for the final round), plus the legendary 'Rumble in the Jungle' with George Foreman in Zaire in 1974, which he won in the eighth round, against all the pre-fight predictions, with consummate ringcraft and great courage under fire.

At the height of his powers Ali had a bewildering speed of hand and feet, an athletic elasticity (one opponent said he never knew any fighter who could stretch so far back over the ropes to avoid being hit), a dancing mobility and an array of virtuoso tricks — the "Ali shuffle" that left giants floundering as their punches missed their target helplessly, the "rope-a-dope" in which he covered up with his arms and gloves and allowed opponents to tire themselves out by battering away to little effect, and the non-stop rants of mockery, before and during the fight, that maddened and confused them.

He was never an orthodox boxer, often taunting his man by keeping his hands low around his hips, inviting a punch then either swinging his head to avoid it or dancing away.

Such daredevil tactics required a level of fitness and fight preparation that were magnificently evident in his early years, but slowly diminished in time, especially after the three-and-a-half year lay-off between 1967 and 1970 caused by the jail sentence (which he never actually had to serve) and the legal battles he faced for refusing the draft to serve in Vietnam.

He was stripped of his world title and refused a licence to box in any state. Some shrewd judges believe that, because of that enforced absence from the age of 25 to nearly 29, the world never saw the very best of Ali. He was never beaten before 1967, having had a run of 29 successive victories, 23 by knock-out, since turning professional in 1960 at the age of 18. After his return to the ring in 1970 until his retirement eleven years later, he suffered five defeats, though three of those were to inferior fighters as he stubbornly fought on, against medical advice and in poor physical shape, until a month before his fortieth birthday.

The only men to beat Ali in his prime were Ken Norton, who broke his jaw in 1973, and Frazier; and he took his revenge on both men twice in the return bouts. In his whole career he won 56 out of 61 fights, 37 by knock-out. At six feet three he was taller than most of his challengers and used his height and exceptional reach, 80 inches, to fend off aggressive opponents. His best fighting weight was about 210 pounds (just under 15 stone), which is not heavy by modern standards.

Cassius Marcellus Clay Jnr was born in the West End district of Louisville, not the city's most deprived area, on January 17th, 1942. His father was a sign-writer with artistic ambitions and his mother a domestic servant. Because his parents had jobs, owned their own house and had only two children, the young Cassius was not brought up in the desperate poverty that fired the ambitions of many black fighters at the time.

His father was a loudmouth (a trait inherited by his elder son), a drinker and a womaniser. The names of both father and son derived from a nineteenth century white Kentucky farmer and soldier who became an abolitionist and freed his own slaves. The future fighter's great-grandfather worked for Clay and passed on his name and may have been a freed slave himself. His mother had some white blood, including that of an Irish grandfather from County Clare who had married a black woman.

When he joined the Black Muslims (or Nation of Islam, as they renamed themselves) his white blood became an embarrassment — the Muslims claimed all white people were "evil" — though in later life he managed to overcome those scruples and visited his ancestor's home in Ireland.

He took up boxing when someone stole his new bicycle and he reported the theft to a policeman. The policeman was Joe Martin, who ran a boxing club in Louisville which he persuaded Clay to join at the age of 12. He took eagerly to the rigours and disciplines of the sport, rising before dawn for road runs and gym work. Martin was his trainer until he turned pro six years later.

He had a poor academic record at Louisville's Central High School, being ranked 376 out of 391 pupils. This was put down mainly to daydreaming in class. However, the school's Principal, Atwood Wilson, had a soft spot for the talkative boy and introduced him to the school assembly: "Here he is, ladies and gentleman, Cassius Clay! The next heavyweight champion of the world. This guy is going to make a million dollars!"

As an amateur boxer, between the ages of 12 and 18, Clay amassed

100 wins with only eight losses, two national Golden Gloves championships and two national Amateur Athletic Union titles. After the 1960 Olympic Games in Rome, at which he won the gold medal in the light heavyweight division, he turned pro. For this he needed financial backing, which was first offered by a Louisville millionaire. After some time working on the man's estate, however, and being abused as "a nigger" by the family, he took up an alternative offer from a syndicate of 11 of Louisville's leading white businessmen.

He also needed a new trainer. After being brushed off by Sugar Ray Robinson and rejecting Archie Moore (whom he later beat when the former world light-heavyweight champion was 47 and he only 20), he was introduced by one of his backers to Angelo Dundee, the son of Italian immigrants who had handled some serious fighters. Clay went to work in Dundee's legendary Fifth Street Gym in Miami Beach and the two men formed a career-long partnership. Dundee never tried to change the young man's unorthodox style and even encouraged his showmanship.

Court jester in his corner was Drew "Bundini" Brown, who coined his famous slogan, "Float like a butterfly, sting like a bee," and started Clay's habit of forecasting the round in which he would fell his opponent. A noted eccentric, Brown called God "Shorty" and used to say to Clay before a fight: "I've just heard from Shorty. He's on our side."

Also in Clay's corner was Ferdie Pacheco, who became his doctor. Pacheco said of Clay: "In 1961, 1962, 1963, he was the most perfect physical specimen I had ever seen…perfectly proportioned, handsome, lightning reflexes and a great mind for sports."

Pacheco was later to resign when the boxer, by then in his thirties and starting to show the effects of taking too many punches, refused his advice to retire before he suffered permanent injury.

By 1964, after four years as a pro, Clay had won 19 straight fights, all but four them by knockouts, and was ready to challenge for the world title. He had already acquired a reputation for his big mouth — "Gaseous Cassius" and "the Louisville Lip" were two of his nicknames. He started baiting the current holder, Sonny Liston, calling him "a big ugly bear" and following him around to throw more insults. Liston, a convicted hoodlum in the pocket of the Mafia, was an uncouth bully who was portrayed in the press as a beast, a frightening black bogeyman.

An early attempt by promoters to present Clay as a contrasting "good nigger" (America was still a segregated society, remember, only in the early days of the civil rights movement) was sabotaged when the contender was pictured in the presence of Malcolm X, the radical Black Muslim leader who was one of the most feared and despised figures among American whites. He then announced that he was joining the sect himself and would henceforth be known as Muhammad Ali, rejecting the name of the "colonialist slave-owner" with which he had been baptised.

His interest in black politics was nothing new. He had been greatly moved by his father's enraged account of the lynching of a 14-year-old black boy, Emmett Till, in Mississippi in 1955. His father had also told him about Marcus Garvey, the apostle of Black Pride. He himself had been upset by the evidence of segregation in Louisville, especially when his mother was refused a drink of water in a whites-only café. He started going to the rallies of Elijah Muhammad from 1959 and befriended Malcolm X in 1962.

A religious man who prayed several times a day to the end of his life, he was impressed by the personal morality preached (but not always practised) by the Black Muslim leaders. In 1975 he became a Sunni Muslim and towards the end of his life, in retirement on his farm in Arizona, he practised the spiritual exercises of Sufism. He had four wives, seven daughters and two sons, one of them adopted. One daughter, Laila Ali, became a professional boxer.

Although he had always belittled his opponents before a fight, often in home-made verse, his rants against Liston were the first time the boxing press had heard the insults at close quarters. Most wrote them off as the ravings of a lunatic, especially when he raged at Liston so wildly at the weigh-in that doctors found that his blood pressure had doubled.

Clay explained to friends that his aim had been entirely rational: to get inside Liston's head, to get him to think of the contender as an inconsequential clown. "He knows how to handle a fighter," he said, "but not how to handle a nut." A writer for *Sports Illustrated* said: "Ali had the capacity almost of self-hypnosis or self-induced hysteria and he'd work himself up to this crazy pitch."

Floyd Patterson, a former world champion beaten by Clay, once said: "I never liked his bragging. It took me a long time to understand who Clay was talking to. Clay was talking to Clay." His ravings have been likened to a Red Indian or Maori war dance: to intimidate his opponent and bolster his own self-belief.

It worked with Liston, whom he beat in six rounds (and the return bout in one), just as it worked with most of the opponents that followed. He was particularly cruel in his taunting of Frazier ("It will be a killa…and a chilla…and a thrilla…when I get the gorilla in Manila," he had chanted) yet he admitted when the man died that he had really admired him. His approach to a fight was largely psychological, working out how to confuse his opponent.

But he was also a shrewd boxing technician, studying his opponent's style and how best to counter it. In his later years, when the speed in his legs had gone, he had to learn how to absorb heavy punches. In the end, tragically, he took too many punches for his own good.

The man who was despised in the 1960s for dodging the draft was later sent by the President of the United States to visit war-zones in Iraq and Afghanistan, where he was welcomed by soldiers as one of his country's great heroes. His stand against the Vietnam war encouraged Martin Luther King to lead a black revolt against it. His reason for not fighting caught a growing anti-war feeling in the country: "I ain't got no quarrel with them Vietcong. No Vietcong ever called me 'nigger.'"

One reason why Ali became one of the most famous people in the world was that the impact of television in projecting sports contests, and to make its stars unimaginably rich, was just beginning. He became sport's first global TV superstar. But he was not just a vacuous celebrity. He brought a moral element to his fame. The sacrifices he made for his principled stand against the American government over the Vietnam war made him a hero to black people all over the world.

At heart he was a black man who wanted the white world to pay more attention and respect to his people. He certainly achieved that, and a good deal more besides.

The *Daily Mail*, 2016

WHEN HENRY HAMMERED THE GREATEST

Old Wembley Stadium was used to dramatic events, from the very day it opened for the FA Cup final of 1923, when the legendary policeman on a white horse had to clear the crowds to allow the match to begin. Its most historic day was to come 43 years later when Bobby Moore's England carried off the World Cup.

Three years before that, however, on the night of 18 June, 1963, one of British boxing's greatest-ever coups was enacted there when Henry Cooper knocked Muhammad Ali (then called Cassius Clay) to the canvas with "Enery's 'ammer," a blistering left hook, the first time the future world champion had ever been floored.

It tells us something about the level of the nation's ambitions that that punch is regarded as one of the high spots in British sport, still selling as a commemorative photo nearly 50 years on — even though Cooper, blinded by the bloodied mess that had been his face, went on to lose the fight in the next round. We do love a heroic loser. Dunkirk all over again.

By some accounts, though, Henry shouldn't have been a loser that night. As Ali reeled from the killer punch, his armpit caught in the ropes and his glove became entangled. He sank slowly to the canvas, as one writer put it, "like a carelessly thrown sack of potatoes." Had he not got caught up in the ropes, his head would have hit the canvas with a thud that might have laid him out. At the count of four, the bell rang for the end of round 4 and he got up and tried to stagger to his corner — "doing a fair impersonation of Groucho Marx's walk," according to one observer.

Ali's canny trainer, Angelo Dundee, steered him to the corner, which was illegal, and later admitted to tugging at a tiny tear in the glove (which was even more illegal) and calling for a replacement, which took at least a minute to arrive. By this time he had applied smelling salts to his boxer, which was also illegal, and restored him to his senses. Never a man to bear grudges, Cooper spoke philosophically about this episode: "There was undoubtedly some crafty corner work, but I expect someone would have done the same for me."

Ali then went out in the fifth round with both hands blazing and blasted at the scar tissue thinly protecting the notoriously weak area around Cooper's eyes until the referee had to step in to save further bloodshed. One writer said after the fight: "There hadn't been so much blood in the London prize ring since the inception of boxing." Cooper was actually ahead on points at the time. Since that fight a spare pair of gloves has to be kept in each corner. Cooper was two stone lighter than his opponent and had prepared for the fight of his life without the benefit of a trainer.

Ali, not surprisingly, puts a different gloss on events in his memoir. "I dropped my guard and glanced down at ringside at a screaming woman — Elizabeth Taylor, with her husband, Richard Burton — and suddenly something exploded against my jaw". So it was all Liz Taylor's fault. Ali paid tribute to the power of the punch, though, recalling 40 years later that "Cooper hit me so hard my ancestors in Africa felt it."

From that moment "Our 'Enery" was taken to the people's hearts and over the years grew into a national treasure. An honest man in a dirty business, Cooper deserved the accolade, moving with affable ease from sport to showbusiness after he retired from the ring, charming television audiences and the profitable after-dinner speaking circuit until deafness cut back his appearances. He was given an OBE in 1999 and a knighthood a year later from the Queen and a Papal knighthood from the Vatican (he had become a Roman Catholic when he married his Italian wife, Albina) for services to boxing and for the extensive work he did for charity.

Cooper was the first person to win the BBC Sports Personality of the Year award twice (in 1967 and 1970) and is one of only three double-winners in the award's history — the others are Damon Hill and Nigel Mansell. He was a popular chairman of the TV quiz show, A Question of Sport, and famously advertised an aftershave and a well-known breakfast cereal. More recently, he fronted a National Health Service campaign to persuade older people to get flu vaccinations — "Get Your Jab in First!" Henry played serious golf, running pro-am and celebrity tournaments until his old age.

He won 40 of his 55 professional fights between 1954 and 1971, becoming British, Commonwealth and European heavyweight champion. Most of his losses were in the early years and he got better with age and experience. His scalps included Zora Folley, Brian London, Joe Erskine, Billy Walker and Jack Bodell. He is the only British boxer to have won three Lonsdale belts in defence of his crown.

After his epic fight with Bodell, Hugh McIlvanney wrote this tribute: "Cooper was left, as most of us suspected he would be, with another great night to remember. Anyone who questions his right to it must have spent the past decade on another planet. To establish how exceptional he is it is not necessary to stress the excitement of his punching, the contrast between the gentle charm of his demeanour outside the ring and the violent courage of his performances inside, or the consistency that has enabled him to hold the British title for more than ten years.

"It is only necessary to say that on the brink of his thirty-sixth birthday he left home to train for six weeks, isolated from the family that is the centre of his life. More than anything else, those hours of running in cold Kent dawns kept the old man just young enough to win."

Cooper will be best remembered, however, for his two heroic fights with Ali, the second one for the world title, and for his dramatic and controversial final showdown with his young challenger, Joe Bugner. His legendary knockdown alone had earned him the right to a rematch with Ali, but this took three years to arrange, as the controversial young American was fighting his way to the world championship and then defending his title. Cooper trained hard for the fight, the most important of his career.

By this time, however, Ali's reputation had grown to the point where no-one gave the Briton a chance. Before the fight McIlvanney wrote: "Henry Cooper is the nicest fellow ever to be about to be defeated for the world heavyweight title." When it finally came in May, 1966, 45,000 spectators paid a minimum of twenty guineas each to watch the fight at Arsenal's Highbury football ground. They got six rounds for their money before the brutally disrupted scars around Cooper's eyes made it impossible for him to go on.

Cooper was naturally left-handed but fought awkwardly as a right-handed boxer, rather than as a southpaw. After the second loss to Ali, he was matched against Floyd Patterson, the former world champion, who knocked him out in the fourth round. He then went undefeated until 1971, adding the European crown to his domestic titles with a victory over the German champion, Karl Mildenberger. In his last fight he put his British, Commonweath and European titles on the line against the rising British star of Hungarian descent, Joe Bugner.

After a fight in which the ringside judges found it impossible to tell the two men apart on the scorecard, the referee, Harry Gibbs, gave the fight to Bugner by a quarter of a point, the smallest possible margin. The audience disagreed and booed loudly. The commentators mostly disagreed too. Harry Carpenter asked: "How can they take the man's titles away like this?" Cooper, who was hugely disappointed and didn't speak to Gibbs for many years afterwards, believed the verdict reflected the British boxing establishment's view that the sport needed a younger champion. He decided it was time to lay down his gloves and retire at the age of 37.

Henry and his identical twin brother George (born 20 minutes later) were brought up on the Bellingham estate in south-east London and went to school in Lewisham. (The Bedser twins, Alec and Eric, who excelled at cricket, were also born in south London, 16 years before). The twins learned to box by looking after each other in the playground. Henry once said: "We were always very close. We went to school together, we went boxing together, we were together in the Army. We look alike, we think alike, in temperament we're similar and often we catch ourselves repeating the other's remarks" (a habit shared with the Bedser twins).

The boys were naturally talented at sport, especially football and cricket. But once they had been persuaded by a neighbour to join Eltham Boxing Club in 1949, they never looked back. Henry won 73 out of 84 amateur fights, became British amateur light-heavyweight champion at 18 and represented Britain at the 1952 Olympics in Helsinki.

When the brothers turned pro on their twentieth birthday in 1954, they came under the benevolent management of Jim ("The Bishop") Wicks, with whom he they formed a long and friendly relationship. Wicks always refused to allow Henry to fight "that bad man," Sonny Liston. He once said: "I would not allow 'Enery into the same room as him, let alone a boxing ring." George lost 14 of his 30 professional fights and retired after ten years, becoming Henry's corner man and a trusted confidant. He was said to have been a stronger puncher than Henry, but was hampered by a badly broken thumb early in his career.

Henry's wife, Albina, died in 2008 and George in April last year. Henry leaves two sons.

As a boxer, Henry Cooper will be remembered below Lennox Lewis but alongside other British heavyweight champions such as Tommy Farr, Bruce Woodcock, Frank Bruno and Joe Bugner, who were the best of their time but never quite fulfilled their fans' hopes and expectations. In Cooper's case, however, his reputation will be overlaid by his popularity as a truly gentle giant whose career unfortunately provided proof of the toughest old adage in sport: that nice guys tend to come second.

The *Daily Mail*, 2011

ONE OF LIFE'S GOOD PEOPLE

Cliff Morgan was one of the greatest fly-halves of all time and a man much loved wherever rugby is played in the world for his warm and generous personality. He spent 30 years in broadcasting, becoming Head of Outside Broadcasts at BBC Television, and his lilting Welsh tones enchanted millions of households during his 11 years as presenter of 'Sport on 4' from 1987 to 1998.

Even now, 15 years on, his summary sacking by the BBC on the grounds that he was too old-fashioned and too romantic about sport, remains inexplicable. I swear I can still hear his warm, melodious voice, roughened a bit by years of cigarettes. His departure caused one of the most angry listener revolts in the corporation's history.

Looking back, one can see that Morgan's sacking by the BBC was a turning-point in the coverage of sport. He went because some hard-nosed young fogeys had decided that sport wasn't about romance or nostalgia anymore, but about commerce and celebrity. Cliff's credo, which in the end condemned him, was that "rugby is all about toughness, bravery and romance — and I'm old-fashioned enough to believe that sport is all about emotion."

His most famous moment on the rugby field came on the British Lions tour of South Africa in 1955, when he played a starring role in the Springboks' first defeat since the Second World War in an epic match at Ellis Park, Johannesburg. The Lions won 23-22 in what has been described as "without question one of the greatest Test matches ever played anywhere in the world in any era".

Clem Thomas, later captain of Wales, who played in that game, recalled: "Cliff Morgan weaved some of his magic. I can still see him sticking his neck out and rocketing past the great Basie van Wyk with a devastating outside break to score an inspirational try". A local rugby writer said afterwards: "Cliff Morgan is the best fly-half to have played in South Africa in the past 50 years. I have yet to see his equal". Sadly, Morgan's dazzling runs have come down to posterity only in jerky black-and-white newsreel clips.

A contemporary described his "passionate urgency" on the field, "with the ball held at arm's length in front of him, his tongue out almost as far, his bow legs pumping like pistons, eyes rolling, nostrils flaring." At 5ft 7ins and 12 stone, with dark Celtic looks, stunning acceleration and a jinking sidestep, he was an Identikit fly-half in the great Welsh tradition tradition — a line to be followed by Barry John, Phil Bennett and Jonathan Davies.

John once wrote: "The fly-half's job is complex, a jigsaw where cunning, skill, awareness, daring, courage and more than a little arrogance are all part of the make-up". Morgan, by common consent, had all these attributes in spades. It was once said of him that he had "an agility that made Harry Houdini look arthritic". He played 27 times for Wales between 1951 and 1958 and went on two tours with the British and Irish Lions.

Of his first international against Ireland in Cardiff, Morgan recalled: "I felt a a hand gently touch my shoulder. It was the man I was having to mark, the maestro Jackie Kyle. He put an arm round me and whispered as fondly and genuinely as an uncle would: 'I hope you have a wonderful, wonderful first cap today, Cliffie' ". Frank Keating wrote of this episode: "Thus, like all true romances, was the baton passed on". Kyle, who became a missionary in Zambia, has described Morgan as "the best fly-half there can ever have been, thrusting, darting, always unexpected".

Clifford Isaac Morgan was born in Trebanog in the Rhondda Valley on 7 April, 1930, into a nonconformist mining family devoted to chapel and choir. His early years were dominated by both and helped to form his character. Music remained a lifelong passion and he was never happier than when singing with the London Welsh Male Voice Choir, of which he became President.

At Tonyrefail Grammar School he came under the influence of an inspirational teacher, E.R. "Ned" Gribble. Morgan said of him: "He changed my life. He converted me from being a 'soccer-mad Joe', as he referred to me, to a game he loved, coached and understood. He saw to it that his charges developed a deep and abiding passion for the game which, he claimed, 'sweats the vice out of you'. He was a gale of humanity and cared for standards of performance, skill, behaviour, discipline and fair play" — all qualities for which Morgan himself became noted, both on and off the playing field.

With Gribble's encouragement, Morgan moved from school to village rugby, turning out on a windy hillside for Coedely Coke Ovens XV at Llantrisant. "Before the game we had to drive a herd of cows from the pitch; there was little we could do about the cow pats. That is how we learned to swerve and sidestep. Those who failed to develop these skills smelled horribly for weeks".

He was soon talent-spotted for Cardiff, where — in the days long before professionalism — he used to arrive by double-decker bus with his boots, cleaned by his father, in a brown cardboard case. His father had given him a copy of a rugby manual by Wavell Wakefield, the former England captain, which he treasured all his life.

He made his debut for Wales at the age of 21 in that 3-3 draw with Jackie Kyle's Ireland. When, the following year, Wales won the Triple Crown by beating Ireland in Dublin, Morgan senior became so excited that he spat his false teeth fifteen rows in front and never saw them again. His mother said to Cliff: "You are no longer ours. You belong to everyone now".

Morgan resisted the temptations of rugby league. One chairman arrived at his parents' terraced house in a white Rolls-Royce and placed £5,000 in white fivers on the kitchen table, along with a cheque for £2,500. His mother, a powerful figure, said money wasn't important and she wanted her son to stay at home. She cooked the chairman breakfast, then sent him on his way, saying: "It's been lovely to have you down here, but on Sundays we go to chapel".

After retiring from rugby, Morgan joined the BBC, first as sports organiser for Wales, then moved to London as editor of 'Sportsview' and 'Grandstand'. From 1964-66 he was producer of 'This Week' for independent television, working with luminaries such as James Cameron, Ludovic Kennedy and Robert Kee. An unashamed romantic, he once said that for him the greatest pleasures in life were Richard Burton reading Dylan Thomas, a Welsh choir in full song, watching Gareth Edwards play for Wales and working on TV with James Cameron. In 1966 he went freelance.

In 1972, at the age of 41, he suffered a stroke. Alarmed for the future, he and his wife, Nuala, wrote down everything they owned and decided to sell the family car and her engagement ring. They returned money to friends, including a king's ransom offered by Burton. Instead, nursing a slight limp, he rejoined the BBC as Editor of Sport Radio, rising to Head of Television Outside Broadcasts from 1975-87. He was awarded an OBE in 1977 and the CVO in 1986.

He then began his long and popular stint as presenter of 'Sport on 4' that ended with his controversial dismissal. When, on his death 15 years later at the age of 83, the BBC put out a fulsome tribute to Cliff, I couldn't help thinking: "If he was that good, why did you get rid of him?"

He was an outstanding public speaker, often travelling miles to speak free of charge, raising large sums for charities, especially the disabled and mentally handicapped. Audiences warmed to his humour and humility and to his rich fund of anecdotes. I once attended a lunch with him and his old friend Tony O'Reilly, at which the jokes and banter came so fast that one could hardly keep up,

Cliff and I appeared together on a number of sports panels and were once guest speakers at the annual meeting of the Headmasters' Conference. I remember us sneaking out like naughty schoolboys for a quick one. This phase of his life was halted by the onset of cancer of the larynx. It is hard to think of anything more poignant than for a man famed for his voice being silenced in this way.

After his wife died in 1999, he married Pat Ewing, his former head of sport on BBC Radio 4, who brought him great comfort in his last years on the Isle of Wight.

I treasure a letter a friend once showed me in which Cliff had written that I was "one of life's good people." That may not have been true of me, but it was certainly true of him.

The *Daily Mail*, 2013

RUGBY'S GENTLE GIANT

Jonah Lomu was rugby union's first global superstar and arguably the greatest player ever to grace the game. His giant frame — 6ft 5ins and close to 19 stone in his prime — allied with the pace of a sprinter who had beaten 11 seconds in the 100 metres, made him a formidable force as left wing three-quarter for New Zealand.

He played 63 times for the All Blacks, scoring 37 tries. The most memorable of these was one of four he scored against England in the semi-final of the 1995 Rugby World Cup in South Africa, bullocking his way not just past but over and through defenders on his way to the line. The England captain, Will Carling, said ruefully: "He is a freak and the sooner he goes away the better."

Lomu, then only 19, had been a surprise choice for the New Zealand World Cup squad, having won only two caps with inauspicious performances in defeats against France. But the All Blacks coach, Laurie Mains, had seen something special in Lomu's unstoppable displays at the Hong Kong Sevens, where he had run round Australia's legendary winger, David Campese.

He decided to take a gamble on the inexperienced Tongan, a bold decision that was vindicated by the seven tries he scored in the tournament. With the eight tries he went on to score in 1999, Lomu is joint holder with South Africa's Bryan Habana of the record for try-scoring in Rugby World Cups.

A remarkable aspect of Lomu's career is that he performed all his great feats on the rugby field while suffering from a serious liver disease. Although this was only identified as nephritic syndrome in 1996, when he was 21, he had felt the debilitating effects long before and had always had to retire to bed after a game rather than go out on the town with his colleagues.

Although the All Blacks, weakened by a bout of food poisoning, had gone on to lose that 1995 World Cup final to South Africa, Lomu almost won the game for them with a devastating run that beat several defenders, but was halted close to the line by a despairing tackle from the Springbok scrum-half, Joost van der Westhuizen.

At the recent World Cup in London there was a moving scene when the two men greeted each other 20 years after the event – the former All Black with his ongoing liver ailment and the former Springbok in a wheelchair suffering from the late stages of motor neurone disease. Lomu, always a generous man, never resented the loss of the World Cup, recognising that it was an historic moment in South Africa's history.

Lomu had a liver transplant in 2004 but went on playing at various levels of the game until 2007. By 2011 the transplant was failing and for the last four years of his life he was on dialysis for six hours every other day.

His emergence as a superhero at the 1995 World Cup, where he was declared Player of the Tournament, coincided with rugby's formal move into professionalism. His fame had an immense commercial impact. One effect was to persuade Rupert Murdoch that rugby held sufficient attraction to viewers for him to invest millions of dollars in the television rights.

Jonah Tali Lomu was born to Tongalese parents in Pukekohe, a poor area of Auckland, on May 12, 1975. He was taken to Tonga by his parents when he was young to keep him out of trouble after a cousin had been stabbed in a street gang fight in Pukekohe. He later returned to attend Wesley College in Auckland, where he excelled in rugby and athletics.

He started his career as a back-row forward before switching to the wing, which he described as "the best move I could have made." He was the first of the giant wingers who are now a common feature of the game. He was chosen for New Zealand's under-19s and under-21s before becoming the youngest ever All Black at 19 years and 45 days.

He played for numerous clubs at various stages of his career, including the Auckland Blues, the Chiefs and the Hurricanes, North Harbour and Cardiff Blues. He won a gold medal with New Zealand sevens at the 1998 Commonwealth Games and was later inducted into the International Rugby Board's Hall of Fame. He gave his name to several rugby video games.

Lomu had three wives. In 1996 he married Tanya Rutter, a South African, with whom he lived in New Zealand for four years before they divorced. He married his second wife Fiona in a secret ceremony on Waiheke Island in 2003. They divorced in 2008 after he had an affair with Nadene Quirk, causing dissension with her then husband, a rugby player who had married her only ten months before.

In 2012 the couple became members of the Church of Jesus Christ and Latter-day Saints. They had two boys, Brayley and Dhyveille, now aged six and four. Lomu's famous tries from 1995 have been often replayed this year on the 20th anniversary. He recently said about this: "When they show clips of me on TV, my boys turn to look at me."

He died suddenly from a heart attack at the age of 40 soon after returning from a promotional tour in England. His death has brought warm tributes from many international figures in the game, past and present, hailing him as the greatest of players and the most gentle of men.

None would disagree with the verdict of the *Daily Telegraph*'s rugby correspondent, Mick Cleary: "No matter how potent, how fast, how powerful, how slick, how dominant other players have been or will be, Jonah trumped them all."

He once made a poignant remark that hangs over his legend: "Imagine what I could have done healthy."

The *Daily Telegraph*, 2015

ALEX'S DEMONS

The demons that chased Alex Higgins throughout his life finally caught up with him yesterday when he died of throat cancer at the age of 51. Snooker's first superstar, twice world champion and twice runner-up, he ended as a lonely, shrunken, penniless and embittered figure, raging at the unfairness of a sport that had made millionaires of young players with only a fraction of his talent.

At his peak Higgins, nicknamed "the Hurricane" because of his speed round the table, was the most exciting player in snooker's history. "The only true genius I've ever encountered in the game", said six-times world champion Steve Davis. "The greatest natural talent snooker's ever had", according to Ronnie O'Sullivan. Jimmy White, who stayed loyal to Higgins after most friends had given up on him, said he was "the Robin Hood of snooker, a folk hero, a legend".

It is difficult for a modern generation to remember that snooker was virtually dead as a sport before the tempestuous Irishman came on the scene. A few ageing professionals in bow ties and waistcoats played challenge matches in clubs, gently applauded by a respectful crowd. Then came colour television, bringing an explosion of cash and sponsorship and a new and younger audience who wanted something more exciting to watch.

Higgins, the rebel with the tortured face and a repertoire of impossible shots, was the game's first pop star. Like George Best in football and Ian Botham in cricket, he put his sport on the front as well as the back pages of newspapers. "I started the industry of snooker and haven't got much thanks", he used to mutter in later years, and with some justification.

He brought 17 legal actions against the snooker authorities for damaging his career with "unfair" disciplinary sanctions — for offences ranging from head-butting and punching officials, bad-mouthing referees and peeing into flower pots at Wembley — and began a group action against the tobacco companies for ruining his health.

His assaults on his own health were legendary — the additive drinking, fags and drugs, as well as injuring himself repeatedly by falling down. One girlfriend stabbed him and he was accused by a former wife of beating her up.

Higgins was born in Protestant Belfast, just off the Donegal Road, and learned his snooker at the Jampot, a rundown billiard hall round the corner from his home in Abingdon Street. A friend recalls meeting him there for the first time when he was ten and had just bunked off Kelvin School. Alex, he recalls, had a sixpence, provided by his mother and three sisters.

He wanted the friend, who was a few years older, to put threepence on a horse for him while he spent the balance on paying for the light over the solitary table in the Jampot. The gambling became a lifelong addiction too (Higgins loved horses and later made a brief effort to be a jockey at Eddie Reavey's stables near Wantage in Berkshire. It didn't work out because he had a weight problem and was constantly in fights with the other stable lads).

In the Jampot the boy Higgins earned money chalking the cues and marking the score for the older men while he picked up the tricks of the game. "I never had any formal instruction. I learned by watching", he said later. Some of the players he watched were Damon Runyon characters like George "The Bug" McClatchey. Higgins says he learned to play so quickly because a bully called Jim Taylor used to smack him around the head if he was slow.

He was soon recording century breaks inside four minutes and started travelling with a team from the Belfast YMCA. In 1969 they turned up one night to play at the Old Post Office in Blackburn, and the Irishman found himself playing Jim Meadowcroft and the future world champion Dennis Taylor. Higgins, who had arrived with his cue and all his belongings in a plastic bag — for all the world like a gunslinger for hire in the old Wild West — stayed on. They became known as "the three Musketeers".

As Meadowcroft put it, "Alex had miraculously arrived at the club and life on the snooker scene was never to be the same again." He made ten centuries in a single afternoon. Two locals spotted the young man's amazing talent and started managing him, promoting him as Alex "Hurricane" Higgins. Throughout his career Higgins was badly served by managers — largely because the good ones refused to handle him — and one went bust owing him a fortune. Even so, he is said to have wasted £2-3 million.

1972 was the Year of the Hurricane, when the pale, taut, hollow-cheeked ex-jockey turned the world of snooker upside down. He started by winning the Irish professional title, then moved on to the world championship, which was staged in the concert room of the Selly Oak British Legion in Birmingham. There were no television cameras and only one light over the table; even that was hit by power cuts during the Scargill miners' strike.

Spectators, including only four journalists, sat precariously on planks and beer crates. "It was bedlam in there", Higgins recalled, "with chairs being shoved about and pint pots crashing". He beat John Pulman, Rex Williams and then John Spencer in the final. The prize was £480 — less than he later paid in fines — though he had prudently bet on himself over several weeks.

He styled himself "the people's champion" and came across as a moody, mercurial buccaneer with an air of the pool-room shark. His appeal seemed to be that he lived on the dangerous edge. News clippings mounted about his off-table misdemeanours. He lost in the finals of 1976 and 1980, the second time to Canadian Cliff Thornburn in a thriller interrupted by film of the SAS raid on the Iranian embassy.

But he came back gloriously in 1982, beating Ray Reardon with a brilliant final clearance of 135, followed by tears of joy as his then wife Lynn and baby Lauren joined him in front of the TV cameras. That was the high point of his career, the start of a long descent into poverty, violence and disease as he fought a desperate losing fight to retain his form and his family.

For all the excitement he generated at the table, with his gnawing anxiety to win and his ability to conjure up winning shots out of sheer will power, his game — as well as his character — had some fundamental flaws which came out under pressure. He fed off the crowd — "it made him feel like God", says Steve Davis — and when their adoration faltered, he lost confidence.

Technically, according to the experts, he did everything wrong: his stance was square, he lifted his head, his arm was bent and he snatched at his shots. Clive James described him as "a fighter pilot on amphetamines". When his nerve ends were stretched, as they were increasingly as age and his lifestyle caught up with him, his technique let him down and he spent his final years in an undignified scramble to qualify for tournaments against inferior players who could never have lived with him at his glorious best.

The *Daily Mail*, 2010